Robert Maguire & Keith Murray

Twentieth Century Architects

Gerald Adler

© Gerald Adler, 2012

Published by RIBA Publishing, 15 Bonhill Street,
London EC2P 2EA

ISBN 978 1 85946 165 5

Stock Code 75274

British Library Cataloguing-in-Publication Data
A catalogue record for this book is available from the British
Library.

Commissioning Editors: Lucy Harbor and Matthew
Thompson
Series Editors: Barnabas Calder, Elain Harwood and Alan
Powers
Production: Neil O'Regan
Copy Editor: Ian McDonald
Typeset by Carnegie Book Production
Printed and bound by W.G. Baird, Antrim

RIBA Publishing is part of RIBA Enterprises Ltd.

www.ribaenterprises.com

Front cover photo: St Matthew's Church, Perry Beeches
(ceiling), completed 1963

Photo © English Heritage

Back cover photo: Robert Maguire and Keith Murray in
their Kew office 1971. Photo © Architectural Press Archive /
RIBA Library Photographs Collection

Frontispiece: The Lutheran Centre, Bloomsbury, London,
completed 1978

Photo © Keith Murray

Foreword

'Looks rather like a seedy stableyard'. This, according to *London 5: East* (2005) in Pevsner's Buildings of England series, is what Basil Clarke, author of *Parish Churches of London* (1966) noted when visiting St Paul's, Bow Common, for perhaps the first and last time. And, yet there is something rather moving in Clarke's condescending simile. St Luke tells us that Mary 'brought forth her first-born son, and wrapped him in swaddling clothes, and laid him in a manger; because there was no room for them in the inn.'

Not only was a stable the birthplace of Christ, but the choirs of churches, along with schools and colleges, designed by Bob Maguire and Keith Murray from the mid-1950s, were informed and underpinned by a way of building and an aesthetic that owed much, sub-consciously and otherwise, to agricultural buildings. So, perhaps – unwittingly – Basil Clarke was half right.

I must have passed Maguire and Murray's commanding Modern church many times before I ever thought of going inside it. As a boy, I set off – as soon as it was thought tolerably safe – to ride London's buses. Back home from a 'Red Rover' day spent on the top decks or behind the drivers of RTs, RFs and Routemasters, I coloured in streets new to me in soft blue pencil in my well-worn *London A–Z*. Although I had made a point of getting inside every City of London church by Wren and Hawksmoor by the time I started secondary school, St Paul's remained a closed book. I didn't understand Modern architecture at the time, and, in any case, there was no way it could possibly compare to my beloved English Baroque.

And, yet, I did keep turning to look out at St Paul's from the windows of those guards-red buses as they gargled along Burdett Road. Those powerful geometric forms. That confident brickwork. The high lantern. And the words carved into its facades by Ralph Beyer – necessary, perhaps, for the Basil Clarkes of the world – proclaiming 'This is None Other than the House of God', and – just in case I might have mistaken the church for a cockney outpost of Basil Spence's Kensington Barracks, 'This is the Gate of Heaven' above the entrance.

When, as a sixteen year old, I finally passed through this Heavenly Gate, I was taken aback. St Paul's was not the site of a Damascene conversion (on the road to Limehouse), but it was a building that enabled me to connect Modern architecture with what had gone long before it. The great central space was one I linked with the interior of Hawksmoor's St Mary Woolnoth. Perhaps it was perverse to compare Maguire and Murray with the English Baroque, yet St Paul's has remained one of my favourite of all city churches ever since.

opposite: 'Pea-souper', by Robert Maguire, 1951

A later journey, by Tube, took me to St Joseph the Worker, Northolt (1967-69), a church that, with its detached, silo-like bell-tower, sliding timber doors and rugged steel roof, somehow called to mind Hugo Häring's Gut Garkau cowshed (1924-25) at Gleschendorf near Lübeck: here, again, is an agricultural aesthetic, of sorts, seen through an industrial mirror. The same is true for All Saints and St Peter's Crewe (1965). Four years ago I was working in Basingstoke. I spotted what looked as if it might be a church by Maguire and Murray, although it was clearly brand new. This powerful, yet simple design with its great pyramidical stainless steel roof proved to be St Bede's – consecrated in 2007 – by, I was told, JBKS Architects, a firm I didn't know. The partners of the practice proved to be Jeremy Bell and Kelvin Sampson, former directors of Maguire and Co; Bob Maguire worked on the first drawings of this new Hampshire church. It showed.

I have dwelt on Maguire and Murray's churches partly because this is how I first came across their work, but also because – in Britain especially – new churches are rare buildings and ever so hard to get right in a country that is essentially materialist and with precious little time for matters of the spirit. In his book *The Face of London* (1932), Harold Clunn was outraged by the survival of Hawksmoor's 'cube-within-a-cube' City church. 'Why this reluctance', he thundered, 'to sacrifice St Mary Woolnoth when the site must be worth something like £1,000,000, a sum with which so many new churches might be erected elsewhere?'

St Paul's, Bow, proved there could be exceptions to the rule. It showed, too, how rich a seam of design British Modernism could be. At much the same time, or very soon afterwards, inventive architects with a natural eye and sense for history, including Jim Stirling and Chamberlin Powell and Bon, were re-exploring and re-inventing home-hewn Baroque. It must have been impossible for Bob Maguire, Buildings Editor of the *Architects' Journal* from 1954 to 1959, to escape the romantic sentiments and picturesque point of view of the *Architectural Review* that shared its playful Georgian offices, and world-famous basement pub, with the AJ in Queen Anne's Gate. Equally, Keith Murray brought to the practice an Arts and Crafts sensibility that ensured that Maguire and Murray were among the most humane of Moderns.

The September 1983 edition of the *Architectural Review*, published when I was an assistant editor, was devoted to what Peter Davey, the editor, labelled 'Romantic Pragmatism', a form of design by architects who 'have a pragmatic approach to building organisation and construction, and a romantic sensibility.' Maguire and Murray were thought of as Romantic Pragmatists. And, yet, 'romantic' is probably not quite the right word. I went back to look at St Paul's, Bow, before I wrote this Foreword to Gerald Adler's well researched and finely crafted study of the practice. Although a brick building, it has an almost crystalline quality: diamond hard. Rational, yes. Sacerdotal, of course. A muscular composition, it is as well rooted in the tough East London streetscape as it is in the earliest days of the Christian Church some two thousand years ago. Some 'stableyard'.

JONATHAN GLANCEY

Acknowledgements

I am extremely grateful to all those who have offered their assistance and advice to me during the inception, research and writing of this book. It is testimony to the importance that Robert Maguire and Keith Murray put on good client relationships and proper briefing that so many present users of their buildings gave their time freely; I was impressed at how proud they were to be working, studying, or living in a building designed by them, and how keen they were to communicate this to me. So my thanks are due to Gerd Ammann, David Anderson, Darren Barnes, Mark Blandford-Baker, John Church, Steve Clapham, Steve Dyer, Peter Henderson, Sue Keeling, Simon Mackenzie, Sara Novakovic, David Paton, Alasdair and Margaret Paterson, Nick Rodgers, Jon Roycroft, Andreas Schäfer, Kishore Seegoolam, Alma Servant, Maureen Shettle, Kim Stapff and Simon Winn. My entrée into the work of Maguire and Murray began with the church at Bow Common, so my particular thanks are due to Duncan Ross, current vicar of St Paul's, Charles Lutyens, and David Gazeley, Managing Director of Watts & Co.

Architects working for Maguire and Murray have proved most forthcoming, supportive and generous with their time and memories, and I am indebted to George Batterham, Jeremy Bell, Alan Berman, Brian Hendry, Andy Parfitt, Kelvin Sampson and John Waldron for their time and conversation. My thanks are due in particular to Ekkehard Weisner for convening a Maguire & Murray reunion on my behalf, and to Robin Bishop for his expertise and advice in respect of the 'School' chapter.

I must thank Alan Powers, series editor, for agreeing so readily to the idea for this book, and for his support ever since, and Elain Harwood, co-editor, for her support and encouragement. English Heritage has ably supported the project, and particular thanks are due to Charles Walker for the hours spent scanning photographs and drawings. The team at RIBA Publishing has been fantastic; my thanks are due to Lucy Harbor, the original commissioning editor, and to Matthew Thompson, publishing manager, who assumed Lucy's role when she went on maternity leave. I am most grateful to Matthew for his encouragement and sound advice. Sue George has been an astute, helpful, and understanding production editor, to whom I am particularly grateful for guiding an author new to the world of publishing through a thicket of potential pitfalls. Thanks, too, to Neil O'Regan, production controller at RIBA Publishing, for his sterling work on the book.

The University of Kent has been particularly supportive of this project. I am most grateful to Karl Leydecker, Dean of the Faculty of Humanities, to Don Gray, Head of the Kent School of Architecture (KSA), and to all my colleagues at CREAte – the Centre for Research in European Architecture. Brian Wood and Bamidele Ojo at KSA have done magnificent work in keeping me supplied with excellent scans. I am most grateful to the

University for granting me research leave during spring term 2011 to enable me to write up this book. The production of this book has been generously supported by the Mark Fitch Foundation, the Golden Bottle Trust, the King's School, Canterbury and Mark Whitby.

Friends, colleagues and others have enriched my knowledge of the partnership: I am very grateful to Martin Boesch, Chris Charlesworth, Stephen Donald, Tim Gough, Stephen Proctor, Walter Rolfes, Joseph Rykwert, Andrew Saint, Rainer Senn, Colin Stansfield Smith and Austin Winkley for their assistance in filling in gaps in my knowledge. I am very grateful to Edward Bottoms, archivist at the Architectural Association, London, for drawing my attention to material under his purview. Many thanks to Jonathan Glancey for writing the Foreword.

The families of Maguire and Murray have been generous with their time, memories and archives. I never had the opportunity to meet Keith, so the Murray family has been invaluable in its support: thank you so much, Susan Murray and Esther Fendall. Getting to know Robert Maguire and his wife Alison has been a great gift. Bob is a marvellous raconteur, generous with his time, and unstinting in his desire to assist me in recounting the story of his practice and of his long friendship and professional association with Keith. I can look back with fondness to our meetings, and am grateful to both Bob and Alison for their hospitality, in Ettrickbridge, and in Pimlico.

Last but not least I am most grateful for the love and support of my own family during months of M&M-ing; to my daughters Hannah and Becky for their forbearance while my attention has been elsewhere, and to my wife, Lucy, for her support in sustaining me, and for keeping a watchful and critical eye over my writing as it has progressed.

TWENTIETH CENTURY SOCIETY

C20

Without the Twentieth Century Society an entire chapter of Britain's recent history was to have been lost. It was alert when others slept. It is still crucial!

Simon Jenkins, writer, historian, journalist

The Twentieth Century Society campaigns for the preservation of architecture and design in Britain from 1914 onwards and is a membership organisation which you are warmly invited to join and support.

The architecture of the twentieth century has shaped our world and must be part of our future; it includes bold, controversial, and often experimental buildings that range from the playful Deco of seaside villas to the Brutalist concrete of London's Hayward Gallery. The Twentieth Century Society joined this collaborative series of monographs as part of its campaigning work. We seek to research the work of key architects of our period, to offer an enjoyable and accessible guide for novice and enthusiast, and to use the books to help make the case for why these buildings should be conserved.

Previous volumes in the series have already had a major impact. Our nomination of "British Brutalism" to the 2012 World Monuments Watch was successful in part due to Alan Clawley's *John Madin* focusing on Birmingham's Central Library as this architect's outstanding work. The recent Oxford Dictionary of National Biography has also followed our lead and included entries on Donald McMorran (of *McMorran & Whitby*) and Gordon Ryder (of *Ryder & Yates*).

We propose buildings for listing, advise on restoration and help to find new uses for buildings threatened with demolition. Join the Twentieth Century Society and not only will you help to protect these modern treasures, you will also gain an unrivalled insight into the groundbreaking architecture and design that helped to shape the century though our magazine journal and events programme.

For further details and on line membership details see *www.c20society.org.uk*.

CATHERINE CROFT
DIRECTOR

Introduction

Among architectural partnerships, Robert Maguire and Keith Murray were particularly attuned to changes in contemporary society. Their buildings testify to many of the social changes of the era, designed to deal with the straightened circumstances of clients but never appearing impoverished. Owing to Maguire's insistence on cost planning from the outset of a project – not something commonly done at the time – they were intelligently and sensitively handled, getting maximum value from everything that went into the building while avoiding waste.

The buildings were not merely economical solutions to practical problems. Even those not designed for worship have a numinous quality, and schools, housing and university buildings were imbued with an essence transcending the banalities of use. Both partners lived their faith through their work. Robert Maguire never abandoned the Christianity of his family background and Keith Murray's early work as a designer and maker of religious art and artefacts contributed to this orientation.

In line with the avant-garde tendency of their generation, their buildings have a finely judged tectonic quality, a sense that construction matters. Sound and honest construction informed the ethos of economy and spirituality, the judicious blend of pragmatics and idealism that gave meaning to modest projects in the eyes and hearts of clients, users and passers-by.

Maguire & Murray was a practice little known outside architectural circles. The partners would have found self-aggrandising publicity inimical to their ethos of close engagement with the client. As a small-scale practice that resisted the allure of fame and fortune in the dogged pursuit of architectural truth, they were widely admired and emulated and never needed to advertise for staff: students and young architects regarded it as a privilege and an education to work for them. Even though the original partners decided to split up after three decades, their model of a small but high-principled office persisted longer.

The partners were an unusual pair, for while Maguire had a standard architect's education of the time, Murray was a silversmith by training whose work for a well-known firm of church furnishers led him into the world of Modern architecture. John Craig, the partner of Peter Aldington in the practice that became Aldington, Craig & Collinge, the subject of another book in this series, resembled Murray in that he was not an architect by training. The mixed educational antecedents and professional loyalties of Maguire and Murray helped them to challenge the easy assumptions of the architectural establishment, in an age when books such as Ivan Illich's *Deschooling Society*, 1971, questioned the dead hand of the professions. They were though supremely professional, in the sense of being wedded to the vocation of design in pursuit of their clients' needs. They were architects of the Welfare State and its public service ethos, their clients being institutions with strong social agendas and high ideals such as schools, universities and the Church. The world of property developers, luxury villas and corporate headquarters was outside their orbit.

The values of Maguire and Murray were those of the Arts and Crafts Movement in England, with its respect for all kinds of proper making, informed by hand and eye, in the building trades as in pottery, textiles or lettering. The phrase 'nearness to need' used by W. R. Lethaby became their motto, as Maguire explained in his lecture at the RIBA in 1971.[1] Before his death in 1931, Lethaby was scathing about the way that Modern architecture, having attempted to break away from historic styles, had apparently become another style itself. The superficiality of 'contemporary' – the post-war version of Modernism – was the target of the movement of the early 1950s called The New Brutalism, associated initially with Alison and Peter Smithson, and soon afterwards with James Stirling and James Gowan, and a mixture of individuals and larger practices such as Lyons, Israel, Ellis and Gray. New Brutalism was described as 'an ethic not an aesthetic', and strong ethical concerns in English architecture seem to come in cycles, so that similarities can be found in the attitudes and, to a considerable degree, the actual appearance, of Gothic Revival buildings of the 1850s, Arts and Crafts buildings around 1900, and New Brutalist ones of the 1950s.

While never officially incorporated in what at best was a very informally consti-tuted grouping, Maguire & Murray shared the New Brutalist anger at Modernism's loss of energy and direction in the immediate post-war period. In an essay of 1962 Robert Maguire maintained that 'There used to be something loosely called the Modern Movement, "movement" signifying something on the move, developing. The serious contributions to this movement showed the same profound concern, a concern with meanings and values in architecture.' Despite these contributions being 'undis-criminating, biased, self-contradictory, or unrelated to reality', Maguire, and Murray, too, believed that the artistic changes wrought by Modernism, brought about by the profound social, economic and technical developments of the nineteenth and twentieth centuries, were bound to have their effects on the design and construction of buildings and settlements.[2] A focus for Maguire and Murray's frustration – as 'angry young men' in the early 1950s – was Basil Spence's Coventry Cathedral with its liturgically conservative plan, won in competition in 1951 and completed in 1962; this became their bête noire because its novelty only seemed skin-deep. The buildings of the Festival of Britain attracted similar criticism. Churches were the area in which Maguire and Murray made their name and nowhere could ethics be more appropriately exercised. They were not only designers but also deeply engaged in the New Churches Research Group, through which the Liturgical Movement, originating in Europe between the wars, arrived in England with an impact equivalent to that of the Ecclesiological Society a hundred years before in terms of changing the manner of worship in conjunction with the conventions of architecture. For Maguire & Murray, the church became their most well-known building type, and it is largely due to their efforts, through their buildings and writings, that we began to have an authentic expression to the demands of the liturgical movement this side of the English Channel.

Maguire and Murray, as individual designers and together in the practice which bore their names, represented the best qualities of small-scale practice during a timescale that spanned from Harold Macmillan's 'never had it so good' era (whose values they doubted) via Harold Wilson's 'white heat of the technological revolution' (about which they had some reservations) through to the unbridled consumerism of Margaret Thatcher's Britain in the 1980s (towards the end of which their partnership was dissolved).[3] To be acquainted with their projects and writings is of intrinsic architectural interest; their work is additionally an index of the profound social and economic developments that the UK has undergone in the second half of the twentieth century. They believed that architecture had to respond to these external pressures in an intelligent and creative manner, but that the response ought to be tempered by a positive respect for, and engagement with, the human condition. They were not alone in this struggle, among architects and others involved in the arts, as the critic Bryan Appleyard explains in his book *The Pleasures of Peace*.[4] Maguire held that the radicalism of the Modern Movement of the 1920s and 1930s had subsided into the bland stylistic exercise that went by the name 'Contemporary Architecture', that it had 'undergone a premature crystallisation. We have a new *Beaux Arts*. Its success is transforming our cities.'[5] And not for the better, needless to say. The Beaux Arts represented the French academic style and training that Modernism was meant to replace, so Maguire's assertion that Modernism had become the next academic style was quite shocking in the early 1960s. The reduction of much contemporary architecture to thoughtless copying of motifs took its cue from the modern system of architectural education:

> *In almost every architectural school in this country, students are taught to design according to such "principles": garbled versions of a few ideas from the early days of the Modern Movement, applied with an intellectual licence and without understanding. To meet the practical demands of the situation, a whole series of architectural devices had been developed (mostly borrowed out of context from photographs of serious buildings) which appear to answer to these "principles", and are used in various combinations. The constant repetition of these devices gives an appearance of consistency to the products, hence the illusion of style.*[6]

At the same time Murray was convinced that 'material fabric and symbolic pattern' were two aspects of building still within the remit of the architect. He had a similar respect for the early stirrings of Modernism:

> *The revulsion against fancy dress styles of architecture towards the end of the nineteenth century was due to a growing recognition that good architecture can only be created if it is rooted in the life and culture which it serves. Many and varied pronouncements were made as to how an appropriate*

*relationship could be achieved, each concerned with one or more aspects of
the rapidly changing ethos of the age, such as the changing social pattern or
the advance of technology. Among those which have had a lasting significance are the concern for the basic elements of a building – and for function,
in which both architect and client are involved.*[7]

The word 'authentic' characterises Murray's vision for contemporary design, as it
does Maguire's respect for patterns of use and for architectural history. Their designs
invariably arose out of authentic considerations of place, people and construction. In
our postmodern world it is hard to know what is authentic, immersed as we are in
images virtual and meretricious. But it was during the 1960s and 1970s that concerns
started to be voiced about succumbing to the 'hidden persuaders' of commercial imper-
atives – one thinks of John Berger's *Ways of Seeing*, 1972, and Theodor Adorno and Max
Horkheimer's *Dialectic of Enlightenment*, 1944, a book whose ideas were taken up with
alacrity by the post-1968 generation of radical voices. Architectural responses to this
perceived want of authenticity were rarely voiced at the time, at least by practitioners.
It was as if Maguire and Murray were prescient about the severe loss of authenticity
heralded by the postmodern turn in architecture in the 1980s and beyond.

The architect Peter Blundell Jones addressed the problem specifically in a series of
articles entitled 'In Search of Authenticity' in the *Architects' Journal* in 1991–2, while his
American counterpart Michael Benedikt wrote *For an Architecture of Reality* in 1987, a
poetic plea for 'the real' in design practice.[8] The search for the authentic in architecture
has been given greater urgency today, in our hyperreal, virtual world of simulacra.
However, what constitutes 'the real' in our complicated and technological world is
moot: the American art critic Dave Hickey said that he preferred Las Vegas to Santa Fe
because he prefers 'the real fake to the fake real'; indeed, the debate continues to this
day between those pragmatists who broadly accept the given world of technology and
commerce, and those idealists who maintain a critical distance from it.[9] Understanding
the motivations and achievements of Maguire and Murray, who made such a vital
contribution to architectural culture from mid-twentieth century on, can only
encourage and inspire those searching for an architecture of substance and authenticity.
Knowledge of their work, their buildings, projects and writings, informs our debate and
discourse about the direction of architecture today and tomorrow.

Notes

1   Robert Maguire, 'Nearness to need', *RIBA Journal*, April 1971, p.141.

2   Robert Maguire, 'Meaning and Understanding' in *Towards a Church Architecture*, Peter Hammond, (ed.), London: Architectural Press, 1962, p.67.

3   Two recent books by the historian Dominic Sandbrook deal with the changing mores of the period in question: *Never Had It So Good: A History of Britain from Suez to the Beatles*, London: Little, Brown, 2005, and *White Heat: A History of Britain in the Swinging Sixties*, London: Little, Brown, 2006.

4   See Bryan Appleyard, *The Pleasures of Peace: art and imagination in post-war Britain*, London: Faber and Faber, 1989.

5   Robert Maguire, 'Meaning and Understanding' in *Towards a Church Architecture*, Peter Hammond, (ed.), London: Architectural Press, 1962, p.68.

6   ibid., pp.67–8.

7   Keith Murray, 'Material Fabric and Symbolic Pattern' in *Towards a Church Architecture*, Peter Hammond, (ed.), London: Architectural Press, 1962, p.83.

8   Peter Blundell Jones, '1: In search of authenticity', *Architects' Journal*, 30 October 1991, pp.25–30; '2: Tectonic authenticity', *Architects' Journal*, 6 November 1991, pp.32–6; '3: Social authenticity', *Architects' Journal*, 4 December 1991, pp.22–5; '4: Politics of Post-Modern despair', *Architects' Journal*, 8 and 15 January 1992, pp.29–32. Michael Benedikt, *For an Architecture of Reality*, New York: Lumen, 1987.

9   Dave Hickey, 'Dialectical Utopias', *Harvard Design Magazine 4*, Winter/Spring 1998: cited in George Baird, '"Criticality" and its Discontents', William S. Saunders, (ed.), *The New Architectural Pragmatism: Harvard Design Magazine Reader 5*, Minneapolis, MN: University of Minnesota Press, 2007, p.146.

1   Humanist Brutalists

In Reyner Banham's *Guide to Modern Architecture* of 1962 one building is described in the same breath as Le Corbusier's pilgrimage chapel at Ronchamp: Robert Maguire's parish church of St Paul, Bow Common, in the East End of London.[1] The photograph taken from the north-west porch entrance shows the font looking like a set-piece illustration from Gordon Cullen's *Townscape*, or one of Eric de Maré's sentimentally evocative photographs of nineteenth-century grit from his illustrations to *The Functional Tradition*.[2] Here is the critic Ian Nairn's entry on it from his 1966 classic *Nairn's London* in full, as his plain but forceful prose perfectly describes the authentically modern yet phenomenally timeless church in London's East End:

> One worth-while new church in a city-region of ten millions, at a time when
> France and Germany have dozens. Make what you like of the implications.
> Anyway, here it is, burningly honest but not aggressive, on a run-down street
> corner (Burdett Road and St Paul's Way) in Stepney. It is completely fresh, the
> perennial force seen again for the first time. Purple brick, a top-lit cube on a long
> podium, with a porch almost detached with quivering letters on it: This is the
> Gate of Heaven. And it is. Not one thing has come out of slickness or a wish to
> be original. Hence it is truly original, like All Saints, Margaret Street, a century
> before. Often locked, but it is worth digging out the keys, for it was built from
> inside out, around a central altar. This is under the cube. Around it lights dance
> on a square iron frame, better than all the copies of parclose screens. Demure
> yet full of fun, reverent yet fully light-hearted: the place seems to heal you.[3]

St Paul's Church, Bow Common, London not only marked the launch of the architectural practice of Robert Maguire and Keith Murray, it was also the most famous and significant parish church to be built in Britain in the latter half of the twentieth century. It crystallised architectural and theological thinking about the form that the church should assume in the post-war era. This important church marks a critical moment in British architecture, poised between progressive attitudes to both design and theology. The buildings of Maguire and Murray are never simply pure exercises in architectural form-making, nor are they aesthetically disinterested essays in response to a client's brief. The balance and equilibrium attained between 'form' and 'content' was remarkable. This story begins with the coming-together of two people from different backgrounds but with shared ideals: humanist Brutalists, to coin an apparently oxymoronic phrase that links the two philosophical and conceptual bases of the advanced architecture of the 1950s.

opposite: St Paul's church, Bow Common: sanctuary

Robert Maguire

Robert Maguire was born on 6 June 1931, in Paddington, London. His father Arthur was a self-taught cabinetmaker; he started with a small workshop, eventually building it up into a business with six employees. His mother Rose Fountain kept the house. His primary education was at Droop Street Primary School, Paddington; in the 1930s it was one of a handful of London County Council schools which experimented in using arts and handicrafts in its general pedagogy, akin to the teaching methods in Rudolf Steiner's system. The experience of his father's workshop and his progressive education would stay with the young Maguire, informing both his choice of future career, and his involvement with it.

With the outbreak of the war Maguire and his sister were evacuated to Newport Pagnell, Bucks., but he was soon on the move again, to Essex, having won an LCC scholarship to Bancroft's School, Woodford Green. He became a boarder at this minor public school, and received a sound education, despite these years (1942–47) being, according

above: Robert Maguire in the Architectural Press boardroom, awaiting his interview for the Michael Ventris Memorial Research Fellowship, 1957

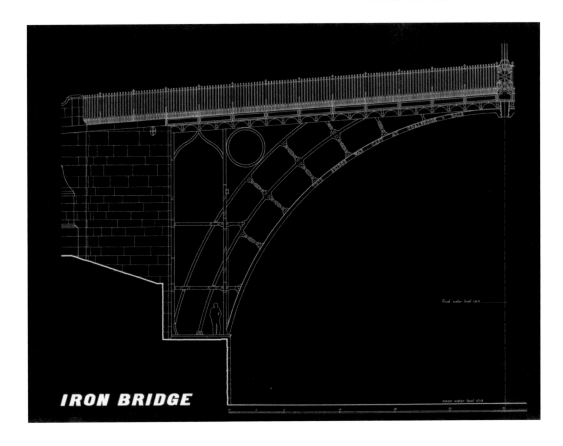

IRON BRIDGE

to him, the unhappiest of his life. At Bancroft's he did woodwork under the tutelage of a Bauhaus-oriented master, and was able to build on the craft skills learned from his father. He left without taking the Higher School Certificate, which was not required then for entry to schools of architecture, instead concentrating on maths and art in the lower sixth. His earlier fantasy of becoming an architect had become more concrete under the influence of his art master, Ray Bradshaw: a cache of old *Studio* magazines provided the raw material, and Maguire would spend his time redrawing plans (largely of Arts and Crafts houses) and reading modern design classics, such as F. R. S. Yorke's *The Modern House in England*, Le Corbusier's *Towards a New Architecture*, Frank Lloyd Wright's *Autobiography*, the constructivist manifesto *Circle* and Raymond McGrath's *Glass in Architecture and Decoration*. The summer after leaving school Maguire got on his bike and saw the 'eight modern buildings' in London at the time: Berthold Lubetkin's Highpoint, Highpoint 1 (1935) and Highpoint 2 (1938); Serge Chermayeff's offices for Gilbey's, Camden Town (1937); two houses in Church Street, Chelsea: Mendelsohn &

above: Robert Maguire's measured drawing of the iron bridge at Coalbrookdale, 1950. The bridge was surveyed by Maguire with Peter Matthews and Jeremy Benson.

Chermayeff (1936), and Gropius and Fry (1936); two in Frognal, Hampstead: Connell, Ward, Lucas (1938) and Maxwell Fry's Sun House (1935); Fry's Kensal House, Ladbroke Grove (1936); and William Crabtree's Peter Jones department store, Sloane Square (1936).

In late 1947, at the age of 16, Maguire began unpaid work for a recently demobbed architect, Laurence King (1907–81) who specialised in church buildings and furnishings. As the sole draughtsman, he drew every job that came through the office, supplementing this 'learning on the job' by enrolling in an evening course at the Northern Polytechnic. Here he learned the finer points of draughtsmanship: watercolour rendering, casting shadows, perspectives, and so on. By this time Maguire realised that only one school of architecture would do for him: the Architectural Association (AA) in London. It was the only one (at least in London) where the Modernism redolent of the 'eight modern buildings' was being actively pursued. The only way he could possibly attend was by winning the one annual scholarship – the Leverhulme – which he duly did, thanks to his drawing skills, and his rapidly developing interest in, and knowledge of, Modernism.

Maguire's stint at the AA was a continuous five-year period, from 1948 until 1953. On arrival he discovered that he was one of only three 17-year-olds, with the great majority of students being demobbed men and women from the services in their mid to late twenties. The young Maguire was seated – no choice in those days – next to Michael Brawne and Jake Nicholson, the eldest son of the painter Ben. The friendship with Jake served to expand Maguire's social, cultural and geographical horizons. Soon he was

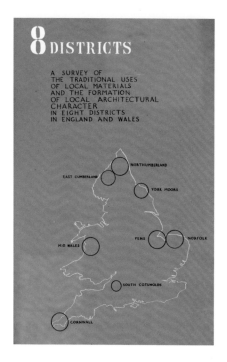

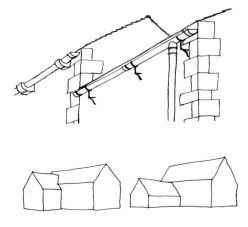

left: '8 districts' report, Robert Maguire 1949, flyleaf
above top: '8 districts' report, sketch of Cumbrian 'clipped eaves'
above   sketch of building form responding to lack of availability of lead for valleys (N Yorks)

holidaying in the Cumberland Fells, staying at Boothby, the house occupied by Jake's mother Winifred Nicholson and her widowed father Charles Roberts, and brushing up against Modernist artworks and objects of craft design. The AA that Maguire found himself in was changing quite rapidly. The new Principal, Robert Furneaux Jordan, developed the idea of group working, simulating in many respects the collegiate atmosphere of the more progressive practices of the day, notably the young, post-war practices of many of the part-time tutors. Maguire worked with Michael Brawne, Michael Cain, Paul Hamilton, Peter Matthews and Jeremy Benson. Indeed, his final diploma project, for a new prestressed concrete bridge next to the famous Ironbridge in Shropshire, was done jointly with Peter Matthews. A particular change Maguire remembers, beginning

top: **Two sketches from '8 Districts' report, farm buildings and dry stone walls. Robert Maguire, 1949**

with his second year, was the move to drawing on tracing paper, as opposed to working painstakingly on stretched hot-pressed paper.

He proved to be a precocious student at the AA, and was awarded the Howard Colls Travelling Studentship for his first year portfolio. Ever the keen cyclist, he decided to undertake a grand tour of selected districts of England and Wales, producing on his return the report *8 Districts*, an elegant collation of notes and observations, illustrated by photographs and simple line drawings with applied colour-wash. This study, which included the fells around Boothby in Cumberland, was an early homage to the vernacular *avant la lettre*, predating the later productions of Ronald Brunskill, Alec Clifton Taylor and John and Jane Penoyre. It convincingly related building form to topography and geology, and was precise and accurate about building material, form and junctions. These two strands, of European Modernism garnered at the Nicholson household and of a pragmatic British rural romanticism, of abstraction tempered by tradition, would run like threads through his life, affecting his attitudes to design, but also to his views on life generally. These twin threads would draw him to a like-minded individual, his future professional partner.

Keith Murray

Keith Murray was born on 25 March 1929, at Quetta, India (today in Pakistan). His father served in the Indian Army, and his mother was an artist who had studied at the Slade in London. He was educated in England: up to the age of 13 at Stone House School, Broadstairs (relocating during the war to Yorkshire) where his creative and independent

above: Keith Murray, c. 1969

thinking was emphasised, and then at Sherborne School, from 1942–46. Keith curtailed his education, leaving after only one year in the sixth form, to begin National Service from 1947–49. He held the rank of 2nd Lieutenant in the King's Royal Hussars. On leaving the army he found an outlet for his practical and artistic inclinations by joining Watts & Co. as their sole in-house designer. This firm of church furnishers was founded in 1874 by three leading architects of the Gothic Revival, George Frederick Bodley, Thomas Garner and George Gilbert Scott (the younger). Their aim was to set up an establishment which would supply their stylistic requirements in the fields of silverware and other metalwork, fabrics, embroidery and wallpapers. The late Victorian style persisted in the firm's work, but when Elizabeth Hoare, a great granddaughter of Sir George Gilbert Scott, took over with her husband in 1953, a brief period of modernisation occurred, including the employment of the young Keith Murray and the remodelling of their showroom in Dacre Street, Westminster, in a very non-ecclesiastical white emulsion on Miesian walls in concrete blockwork, designed by Robert Maguire.

Keith had two passions, religion and design, in all their manifestations. Both found ready outlets at Watts. He enrolled at the Central School of Arts and Crafts in London, the design School co-founded by the Arts and Crafts architect William Richard Lethaby (1857–1931), who was to be influential for Maguire & Murray, and from whom the practice's slogan 'nearness to need' derives. His evening course was in silversmithing and jewellery which he pursued for two years, by which time he was well established at Watts. Through his connections at Watts and the Central School Keith became acquainted with a number of significant designers and craftsmen, including the silversmith Michael Murray (1923–2005; no relation) and Ralph Beyer (1921–2008), the letter-cutter who would later design the letters on the entrance porch to St Paul's church, Bow Common and those inside the practice's children's nursery in Kreuzberg, Berlin.

above: **Watts & Co, braiding, designed by Keith Murray, 1950s**

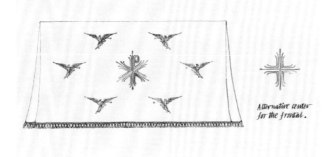

Sketch of a Frontal proposed for an Altar in the Crypt of Rochester Cathedral.

Alternative center for the frontal.

Scale 1½ inches = 1 foot.

Michael Murray was the key figure relating religion with the design crafts in Keith's early career. The locus was the artists' community founded by sculptor and designer Eric Gill (1882–1940) at Ditchling, East Sussex, where Michael was apprenticed to the silversmith Dunstan Pruden (1907–74). Here a heady brew of artistic ferment and the 'smells and bells' of Roman Catholicism and High Anglicanism prevailed. Ditchling was the pre-eminent centre of Catholic-based design and crafts in the country; it fostered a quasi-mystical approach to the making of physical artefacts that was Arts and Crafts in its ethos. It was bound to appeal to the young, idealistic Keith Murray. It was initially through his encounter with Michael Murray that Keith aligned his enthusiasm for

top left: Watts & Co, glass and silver vessels, designed by Keith Murray with Michael Murray, 1950s
top right: Watts & Co, silver chalice, designed by Keith Murray and Michael Murray, 1950s
above: Watts & Co, altar frontal design, crypt of Rochester Cathedral, designed by Keith Murray, 1950s

Christianity with its material expression. At Watts & Co. he came into contact with a variety of clergymen, but in particular with those of a progressive bent who formed a substantial part of the company's clientele. In his discussions with them concerning the design of chalices, vestments and silverware, he became aware of an alternative, modern tradition of craftsmanship which Watts was unique in representing within British ecclesiastical design circles. Keith furthered his combined interest by reading *The Shape of the Liturgy* (1943), by Dom Gregory Dix (1901–52) and by seeing Christian traditions of art and craft outside his own experience of Anglicanism, most notably those of the Orthodox churches. Greece was where he took holidays, visiting churches and monasteries.[4]

Maguire and Murray

In 1952 Robert Maguire met Keith Murray at the flat of a mutual friend. Maguire was in his penultimate year at the Architectural Association School of Architecture in London, while Murray (never an architect, incidentally, neither by training nor qualification) was working as designer at Watts & Co. It was a timely encounter for these two left-liberal, reform-minded young Christian men. Maguire (then still a Roman Catholic) had just failed an AA design project for a church; his tutors could neither understand its non-ecclesiastical appearance, nor did they appreciate his design methodology with its emphasis on the close observation of the movements of both clergy and laity during a reformed liturgy.

Father Groser, a like-minded spirit in matters liturgical and a client of Watts's, invited Murray to participate in a competition, with Michael Murray, for the fitting-out of a new chapel designed to a conventional plan by the architect Roderick Enthoven at St Katherine's Foundation, just east of the Tower of London, and Maguire offered to make the set of drawings in his capacity as a talented draughtsman. They won. The scheme was the first of many church reorderings that Maguire and Murray would undertake in the following three decades. Its hallmark was simplicity, with the focus being on the Eucharistic liturgy, centred on the altar table itself.

At this time Maguire, by then looking for somewhere to live, stayed for a short time with the Michael Murrays in their Bloomsbury house. This stay was significant in putting Maguire in touch with the vigorous continuity of Arts and Crafts practice in contrast to the more refined, 'continental' atmosphere of the AA; this built on the education he had already received courtesy of the Nicholsons. The intermingling of English craft traditions with concerns for the purity of 'functionalist' approaches to architectural design was critical in determining the direction taken by Maguire (and Keith Murray as his partner), a direction different to that of most of his contemporaries. For Maguire and Murray did indeed indulge in applied decoration where it was deemed appropriate, and it was this apparent anomaly, their ability to contemplate decoration, which distinguished them from their then more earnest New Brutalist peers, such as Alison and Peter Smithson, and James Stirling and James Gowan. These architects later softened their attitude from

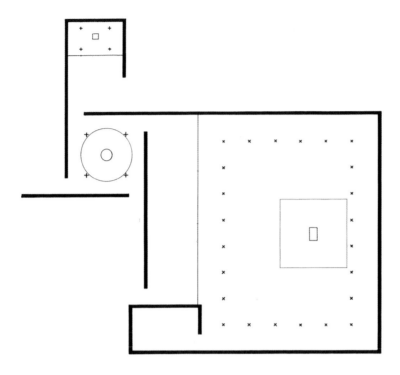

their initial hard-line, dogmatic resistance to any form of applied decoration, on the one hand as a reaction to what they perceived as the fripperies of the Festival of Britain style, and on the other as homage to their hero, Le Corbusier, whom they perceived as doggedly opposed to everything parochial in design. In this, Maguire and Murray were ahead of this particular move. Murray later wrote that 'When we have freed ourselves from aesthetic inhibitions sufficiently to be open to the possibility of decoration, there is still the difficulty that we have in designing in the absence of a valid decorative tradition', and for both men the search for the void left by the absence of such a tradition would define their subsequent practice.[5] At Bow Common, Ralph Beyer's bold lettering on the entrance porch is an example of appropriate decoration on the church, as are the mosaics executed by Charles Lutyens on the spandrel panels framing the space of the sanctuary.

Bow Common

One has to imagine what London was like in the immediate post-war years before the rebuilding boom of the 1960s got underway. The East End, which had suffered most from aerial bombardment, had an air of dereliction. (The feel of austerity London is

above: Robert Maguire, AA 4th year student project, plan of church

described to great effect by Iris Murdoch in her first novel, *Under the Net*, in 1954.) Church buildings had suffered as well, but by the time rebuilding was possible it had been decided to rationalise the Church of England's estate to some extent, often by amalgamating adjacent parishes, as happened at St Paul's, Bow Common. Fr Gresham Kirkby (1916–2006), the vicar of the new parish, was a regular visitor to St Katherine's Foundation, where he met Keith Murray. He styled himself as an 'anarchist communist' until the Hungarian uprising of 1956 when he softened it to 'anarchist socialist', and was ready to experiment in the design of his new church, becoming central in the developing partnership between Murray and Maguire.

The War Damage Commission had decided upon the sum of £50,000 for rebuilding the bombed-out church (to be named St Paul's) together with the generous sum of £8,000 for stained glass lost in the war, which was allowed to be put back in the form of glass mosaics. This commission had been awarded to Murray, who subsequently introduced Maguire to Kirkby; Maguire's credentials were scanty, to say the least. He came armed with a hypothetical church plan he had prepared for publication in Edward Mills's book *The Modern Church* (1956) and his failed AA student church project.[6] The germ of the executed church at Bow Common can easily be seen in these two designs, the first one a bold, flat-roofed composition with a pronounced reinforced concrete diagrid structure, the second with parts more individually articulated, influenced by the planar wall elements of Ludwig Mies van der Rohe's brick villa and Barcelona Pavilion projects of the 1920s, in which the continuous enveloping wall gave the degree of enclosure required in a church.

Maguire had been advised to tone down his proposal by the architects Andrew Carden and Emil Godfrey, principals in Carden and Godfrey, the practice for which he had worked on and off during vacations. In fact, Maguire based his fledgling practice from its office in Chancery Lane, London for three years, until 1958. He had been obliged to go into association with such an esteemed practice in order to assure Archdeacon Michael Hodgins at London Diocesan House that he could – at age 25 – manage this prestigious job. Maguire was persuaded by the avuncular Carden and Godfrey to submit a compromise scheme

above: **Project for a hypothetical Roman Catholic church, Robert Maguire, 1955, prepared for publication in Edward Mills's book *The Modern Church* (1956)**

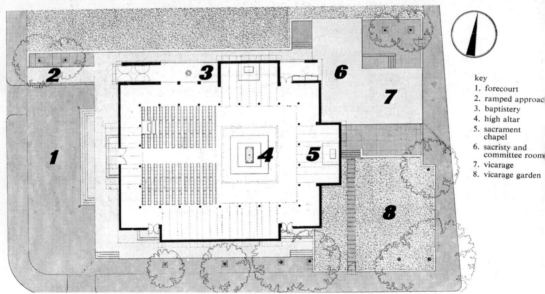

key
1. forecourt
2. ramped approach
3. baptistery
4. high altar
5. sacrament chapel
6. sacristy and committee room
7. vicarage
8. vicarage garden

above: Model and plan of the 'compromise scheme' for St Paul's

intended to elicit the support of the Diocesan Advisory Committee (DAC), an outwardly
– but not inwardly – conservative proposal with a slender spire atop a glass cupola, with
double-pitched roofs apparently defining nave, transepts and eastern apse. They said
to Maguire that he should 'go for the radical thing you want to do but compromise the
outside, to get it through'.[7] However, even in this scheme the characteristic external feature
of the executed church – the folded concrete slab forming the low roof at the periphery – is
in evidence. This is a borrowing from his 4th year AA design project for a foundry. Indeed,
the scheme's simple but bold tectonic expression – simpler and bolder in the executed
church – owes a great deal to the rigorous expectations of an AA student in the early 1950s
in matters structural and constructional. One only has to see his joint final project for the
bridge in Shropshire, where everything was calculated down to the last detail.

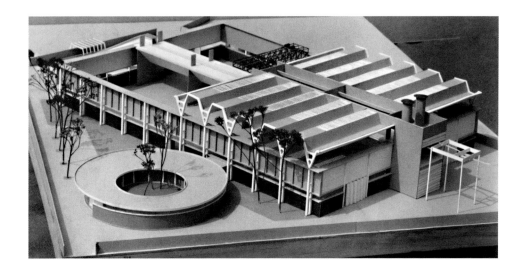

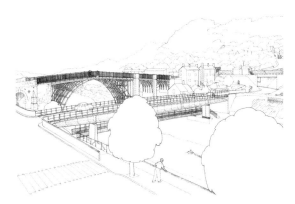

top: Student design for a foundry, Robert Maguire, Peter Matthews and Gordon Sheere, 1951
above: Student design for a prestressed concrete bridge at Ironbridge, Shropshire, Robert Maguire and
Peter Matthews, 1953

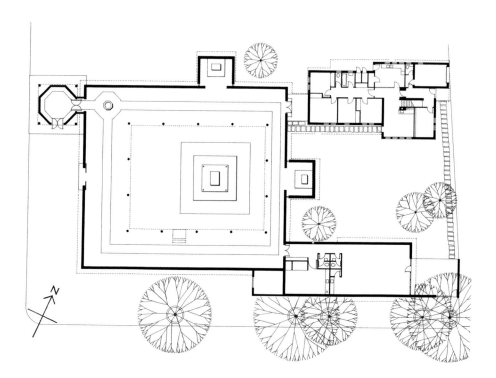

The association with Carden and Godfrey established Maguire's professional bona fides, while the design in its vaguely Festival of Britain pitched-roof manner persuaded the DAC members, classicists Hector Corfiato and Albert Richardson, as well as the Gothicist Walter Godfrey (father of Emil), that it would give the appropriate 'ecclesiastical' stylistic signals. More important for Maguire than the disguise of stylistic clothing was the radical plan he successfully smuggled through, and he still quotes the witticism attributed to John Betjeman on seeing Basil Spence's design for Coventry Cathedral: 'The spirit is willing, but the flèche is weak.'

The weak spire would eventually go, for reasons which beautifully conflate English pragmatism with artistic will. The story goes like this: Maguire's 'day job' at the time was at the *Architects' Journal* as Buildings Editor. Working with quantity surveyors, he had been developing the practice – so familiar to us today – of cost planning, where there is a breakdown of different parts of buildings into elements so that adjustments can easily be made to the budget. One might, for instance, decide to substitute cheaper taps for a more expensive terrazzo floor finish. This expertise proved invaluable when, having received

opposite: St Paul's church, Bow Common: interior view from font. The mosaics in the spandrel panels below the brick box will be eventually executed by Charles Lutyens in the 1960s to the outline scheme of Keith Murray's.

above: St Paul's church, Bow Common, plan, with the vicarage ot the northeast and the vestry and meeting hall to the southeast.

planning approval for the church, the DAC suddenly decreased the budget by 20%, from £50,000 to £40,000. Maguire was able to rejig the design, simplifying its external form, removing the spire and other features, thereby realigning the scheme with his original design intentions. The Archdeacon believed in Kirkby's vision, and this, combined with a simple card model, propelled the project through to completion.

The design of St Paul's, Bow Common, is a curiosity in late 1950s Britain. Some of the stylistic compromises in the scheme initially submitted, such as the traditional Latin cross of nave, apse and transepts, give the impression of a conformist church design of the 1950s, at least as regards its external form. In other respects, the executed design appears to belong in the orbit of 'the New Brutalism', amid the work of the angry young men and women of British architecture.[8] This though would be to miss the point: St Paul's is a 'functional' scheme insofar as it has been designed from the inside out; moreover, the 'inside' is a deeply felt and considered attempt to understand, and in some cases pre-empt, the life of the Church. How people, laity and clergy, actually use the space, and indeed ought to use it in order to relate meaningfully to the life of and in the Church, was the thing which governed its design; with this design Maguire attempted, and succeeded, in finding forms which corresponded more closely than any other church in modern Britain at the time with the 'cult' of the believers within. While none of this characterisation of design conflicts with the Smithsons' definition of Brutalism, the search for authenticity in terms of construction and materials, and a robust response to use and social activities, the fact that it is articulated by Maguire through the vehicle of a church, of all things, is surprising in light of the anti-traditional thrust of Brutalism. One is reminded of the architect Maxwell Fry who, a decade earlier, maintained that 'The vocabulary of modern architecture is capable of enrichment though it lacks the service of an organised and deeply-felt religion.'[9] Adding this to the local deployment of crafts in the executed building leads one to the epithet 'humanist Brutalist' as a means of characterising Maguire's developing practice. Indeed, Alison and Peter Smithson acknowledged that it was '...this reverence for materials – a realization of the affinity which can be established between building and man – which is at the root of the so-called New Brutalism.'[10] Of course this line of thinking is complicated by the divergence between the 'vulgar' and popular under-standing of Brutalism as something mechanical and crude, and the reality of the core movement and its values of honesty, materiality, place, social purpose and strong image. In a sense, all proper Brutalism is humanist at base.

The church is entered from Burdett Road to the west, through the south door of an octagonal brick porch with Ralph Beyer's inscription on the three visible faces of the square flat concrete roof as frieze: TRULY THIS IS NONE OTHER BUT THE HOUSE OF GOD. THIS IS THE GATE OF HEAVEN (the words spoken by Jacob in the Book of Genesis when he awoke after his dream of angels ascending and descending between heaven and earth). The main body of the church mounts up to the east, with a rectan-gular ambulatory, and an overhanging flat concrete roof, a metre higher than that of the porch, bent up into intermittent triangular glazed gables. Then comes a great brick cube (actually, a rectangular cuboid) sitting above the sanctuary; within the sanctuary it is framed by four-bay colonnades to the north and south, and three bays to the east and west. Finally comes the lantern, positioned off-centre with respect to the brick box below, with its truncated pyramid aluminium roof, whose pitch reiterates that of the gabled aedicules at the edge of the church, raised up above vertical walls of glass, with glazing bars forming a pattern of equilateral triangles.

Once one is inside the porch, turning east through a pair of doors, the church proper is revealed. Here the forms perceived externally make sense of the view and experience within. At the edge runs an ambulatory, picked out as a path in brick paviours that stands out from the chequerboard square concrete paving slabs laid throughout, with inset steel grilles delivering heated air. Gresham Kirkby was familiar with the medieval church at Thaxted in Essex, where Conrad Noel, 'the Red Priest', was vicar between the wars, and wanted to reproduce the effect of its unencumbered open floor. Above runs the low, folded concrete roof, with clerestory windows formed in the triangular dips. The ambulatory orders the use, and hence the plan, of the church. The path has one interruption, immediately upon entering the church: the font. This conforms to the traditional place of baptism as the sign of entry into the Church. At its eastern ends the path leads past the only two exits from the church: at the north-east, to the priest's house and at the south-east, to the church hall and garden. Interruptions to the enclosing wall are kept to a minimum, although Maguire's student project suggests that these are not as minimal as he originally wanted. Even so, the enclosing wall is Miesian and uncompromising in its power to impose a strict inside/outside duality on the plan, and the client's needs were seamlessly incorporated.

The church has three significant breaches of the perimeter wall. The central west door is reserved for ceremonial use, a distinction found in many parish churches and cathedrals, although the current incumbent, Duncan Ross, opens the wooden sliding door wide when he wants to welcome the outside world in, and 'show off' the surprising interior. The two other openings are for chapels, one for the reservation of the Blessed Sacrament in a tabernacle at an altar; the second for a Lady Chapel used as a separate chapel for weekday celebrations of the Eucharist.[11] However, Maguire was careful to give the perception that these two chapels were 'outside' the church by introducing vertical slots of glazing that interrupt the U-shape of their enclosing walls. This enhances the focus on the central sanctuary, and ensures that the altar is not compromised in its significance.

Appropriate decoration

The sanctuary itself is framed by the surrounding colonnade; the brick box above is spaced off the colonnade by wing-shaped spandrel panels, decorated by Charles Lutyens (great-nephew of the famous Sir Edwin) with a series of mosaics, paid for out of war damages for lost stained glass. They depict the angels at prayer, with arms raised in the traditional manner, and are reminiscent, in their stylisation and frontality, of Byzantine art so admired by Murray. Furthermore, the pictorial composition makes sense when placed within the shapes of the spandrels, a coming together of decoration and tectonics.

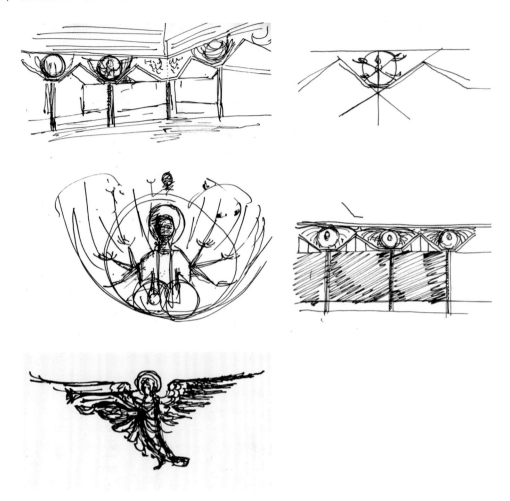

Lutyens executed the mosaics from 1963–68, working to a scheme prepared by Murray who was originally to have executed them himself, but was given a fairly free hand in their design. There are ten angels located in the spandrels, their arms raised aloft almost as if they were caryatids bearing the weight of the lantern above. In the corners the four elements, air, earth, fire and water, are depicted.

The design and location of the altar goes to the heart of what Maguire and Murray were seeking in their rethinking of the church in terms of liturgy. The altar is 'the place of Calvary [as well as being] the table of the mystical banquet – the sacrificial place and the place of communion'.[12] The design of the altar therefore involves an

top left and right: **Studies for mosaics at St Paul's church, Bow Common, Keith Murray**
above: **Study for angel, Keith Murray**

inevitable compromise between its symbolism as the hill of Calvary, the place where the crucifixion occurred, and that of the dining table, most famously depicted as the scene of Leonardo da Vinci's *Last Supper*. The altar sits on a square platform raised two steps up from the general floor level of the sanctuary, in other words, one step less than the usual representation of the hill of Calvary. This is sufficient to make the altar a space apart, while still insisting that it is part and parcel of the sanctuary, located amid the congregation. Two other devices frame and focus the altar: the ciborium or canopy, and the corona or hanging crown above. The communion rail, the 'separating fence', as Murray called it, is entirely absent. The ciborium harks back to Early Christian practice and is a canopy framing the altar. It gives a certain intimacy to the Eucharist service, beneath a tent-like cover with connotations of the temporary. Made of standard steel sections and roofed in two kinds of simple spanning stone, serpentine and white Sicilian marble slabs, it is reminiscent of the ciborium at S. Clemente, Rome, a distant cousin of the Jewish wedding canopy, the *Chuppah*, and the temporary booth known as the *Sukkah*, which forms a focus for festivities at the festival of Tabernacles. It symbolises that, while the crucifixion took place at a specific place (Calvary), one may encounter God anywhere.[13] This strong inward focus culminates in the hanging corona, fabricated again from standard rolled steel sections. The flat bars of the steel structure provide myriad places for candles to be placed. Although not at first obvious, the flexibility revealed by a slight touch shows how this structure related to Maguire's interest in Alexander Calder's mobiles.

Maguire's understanding of functionalism in architecture included fostering and representing the life within. The idea of 'form finding' is amplified to take account of intangible and psychological factors. In the church of St Paul's this means *inter alia* placing the altar in a forward position towards the middle of the church, raised up onto a dais. As Banham wrote in his review of the church:

> *The Liturgical Movement … sets [the architect] a double functional problem to be resolved in a single solution: to create a functional space … to house the priest and the congregation in the celebration of the ritual, and a symbolic space … to house the altar. … This double objective might be achieved by applying symbols to a functional structure, but that would simply be window-dressing. The outcome is only architecture if the functional and symbolical are indissoluble.*'[14]

Function by itself was insufficient for Maguire; he was interested in style, not in the sense of 'the (outmoded) styles' in the manner of Banister Fletcher's history of architecture, but rather in the sense of doing things with style, in a knowing and sophisticated manner. For him it meant continuing and developing the architectural aesthetic of the day. One anecdote must suffice to make the point of Bow Common's contribution to architectural culture. A year after completing St Paul's, Maguire attended a garden party at the Cement and Concrete Association's headquarters at Wexham Springs in Berkshire. He had just designed a path in the garden created by the landscape architect

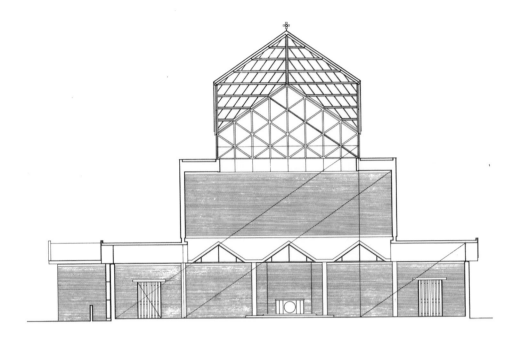

Geoffrey Jellicoe. As they both crossed the lawn, the young James Stirling came over to Maguire and said, 'Maguire, isn't it? I liked that mausoleum of yours, with the crystal thing on top'.[15] A few years later the Leicester Engineering Building was unveiled with its own 'crystalline' glazing to the workshop block.

Rudolf Wittkower was an occasional lecturer at the AA, and his rediscovery of the sacred meaning of Renaissance geometry, explained in *Architectural Principles in the Age of Humanism*, 1949, seemed to Maguire as an idealistic student to be applicable to modern architecture.[16] Wittkower's painstaking exposition of the centralised church plans of Renaissance Italy and their symbolism impressed itself on the young Maguire.

Maguire and Murray believed strongly in a kind of 'deep functionalism', in which close and accurate observation of rites and human movement (those unaffected by architectural form) would lead to rational and effective building forms. Maguire's student church project was developed by means of drawing coloured pencil arrows in different configurations on the plan, representing clergy and laity in procession, or taking communion, and developing these as a kind of choreography of the new, reformed liturgy. The 'new, reformed liturgy' is explored further in Chapter Three, but it was just a means to an end, one which would lead to a well-planned and organically

above: St Paul's church, Bow Common, section with regulating lines, north-south, looking east

organised place of worship; in the end, though, it is not 'movement' as such that the architecture expresses. As he wrote,

> *Architecture articulates and presents meaning, and values; it expresses*
> *these things. It does not 'express' function, because function is not in itself*
> *capable of expression. The underlying meaning and values of 'functions'*
> *– purposes – are, however, capable of expression: capable, that is, of articu-*
> *lation and presentation.*[17]

In Peter Hammond's *Towards a Church Architecture*, 1962, a photograph of the floor pattern of Rudolf Schwarz's church of St Anthony's, Essen (1959) has a caption referring to 'the potentialities of the floor as a means of creating movement pattern [in the manner of] *Townscape* by Gordon Cullen.'[18] Cullen's book, *Townscape*, based on a long-running series of articles in the *Architectural Review*, was published in 1961 and, like Maguire's analysis of movement inside a church, presented urban design as a series of movements and unfolding views, more commonly found in old towns than in new ones. The *Architectural Review* also promoted what it called 'The Functional Tradition', on which a special issue and book by J.M. Richards (with photos by Eric de Maré) were published in 1957 and 1958 respectively, exemplified by nineteenth-century industrial buildings that had the simplicity associated with Modernism, combined with solidity and exposed construction. The elevation of St Antony's, with its array of brick panels and rational windows set into

above: St Paul's church, Bow Common, exterior (the tower block was built by the Local Authority over a decade after the church was built)

a squared concrete frame, shouts 'factory' and announces a large interior volume, since the squares of the frame are too oddly scaled to refer to storey heights.[19] In contrast to the polite architecture normal for churches, St Paul, Bow Common, and the later church, St Joseph the Worker, Northolt (1966–70: see pages 93–96), have tough, industrial connotations ennobled into something of great spiritual significance. Their layouts resonate with the new approach to liturgy, emphasising the reality of the Eucharist and the shared participation of priest and people in worship, coupled with an aesthetic of simple, even banal building, connecting Maguire and Murray to contemporary churches by Rudolf Schwarz, and the younger Swiss architect Rainer Senn (see pages 84–85).[20]

Although the commission for St Paul, Bow Common, was prestigious, it came with a client body constrained by a curtailed budget. Most of Maguire and Murray's clients had similarly limited means and no wish to conceal their position. As Maguire said at the RIBA annual conference at Hull in 1976:

> *... most of the projects which we have been engaged on are at the bottom end of the cost scale and the approach ['to serve life'] suits such work very well; and second because in common with an increasing number of architects and*

above: St Paul's church, Bow Common, entrance porch, with recessed lettering by Ralph Beyer, as restored by the architect John Allan in 2010

other people we feel some emotional difficulty with the idea of building at a
high level of artistic pretention in a world where it is only too obvious that
many people haven't either the food or shelter to keep themselves going. So
we see our job as craft rather than as a fine art and the aim of most of what
we do as the achievement of a high standard of ordinariness.[21]

St Paul's Church, Bow Common, was not only the making of the architectural
practice of Robert Maguire and Keith Murray, it was also the most famous and significant parish church to be built in Britain in the latter half of the twentieth century. It
crystallised architectural and theological thinking about the form the church should
assume in the post-war era. It was a highly symbolic project, the one which would
bring the practice critical acclaim.[22]

'Kentlands', Sevenoaks, 1958

While St Paul's was being built another, far smaller, scheme was under way in rural
Kent, representing the other pole of the practice's work, while sharing Bow Common's
key attribute of ascetism and restraint.

Maguire's 'day job' has already been mentioned, his four-year stint at the
Architectural Press where he functioned as Buildings Editor for the *Architects'*
Journal, and occasional contributor to the *Architectural Review* for its column on
technical innovation. From 1955 to 1957 Maguire contributed to the *Techniques*
series which appeared under the 'Skill' rubric in the back pages of the *Review*,
covering such topics as double glazing, aluminium roof coverings and external
paving. He had also previously collaborated with the architects John Eastwick-Field
and John Stillman on their book *The Design and Practice of Joinery*, published in
1958, for which he produced the clear set of drawings.[23] Then at a meeting in Café
Torino, Soho, Lance Wright, technical editor of the *Architects' Journal (AJ)* and
Architectural Review, had suggested that these technical studies be turned into
a series for the *AJ*. This led in turn to Colin Boyne offering Maguire the job of
Buildings Editor with the *AJ*.

Colin Boyne, the editor of the *AJ* commissioned his young colleague to design a self-
build house for his young family. He had bought a wooded site between Sevenoaks and
Hildenborough, Kent, and as he had never practised as an architect since completing
his training, felt he needed the services of a practical man such as Maguire to advise
him on the pragmatics of detailing and assembly. Boyne's position in architecture
was poised between the picturesque qualities of 'Scandinavian modern' and the more
rugged effects of the New Brutalism. He knew that Maguire was enthusiastic about
contemporary Scandinavian houses, particularly those of the Danish modernists, such
as Jørgen Bo and Jørn Utzon; this reinforced Boyne's decision to ask Maguire to design
the house. The Boynes had limited means; they were at one with Maguire in their desire
for a simple house whose aesthetic arose directly from its palette of materials and
means of assembly.

top left: 'Kentlands', house for Colin and Rosemary Boyne, near Sevenoaks, Kent, view from garden
above left: 'Kentlands', entrance terrace
above right: 'Kentlands', view from living room over raised terrace to garden
top right: Rosemary Boyne on site at Kentlands

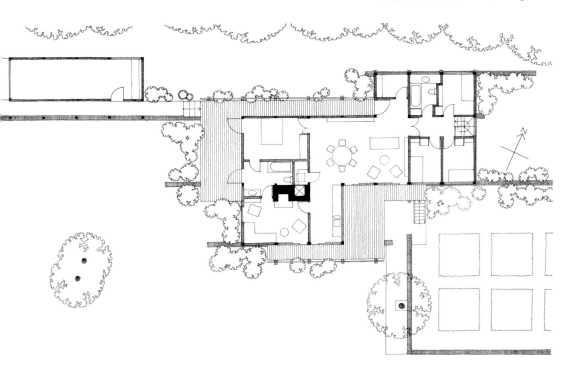

The house was designed to be built in two stages, the children's bedroom wing to be executed when funds became available. The site, though picturesque, was liable to flooding; tall brick sleeper walls raised up the house, and ran out into the landscape. The house is sandwiched between two decks, one to the north, the entrance axis, connecting the garage with the front door, the other forming a wide south terrace. The house plan consists of a rectangular core with a bite taken out forming the semi-enclosed south terrace, with the children's bedroom accommodation to the east. The core is planned in two halves, the family room to the east, a galley kitchen to the south forming the right-angled frame of the terrace, and a parents' domain to the west, comprising main bedroom, en-suite bathroom, and 'snug' to the south. This zone has the chimney, the only brickwork element to protrude vertically through the timber deck from the bearing walls below. Internally, a massive brickwork chimney breast with a hollowed-out fireplace gives onto the snug. Colin Boyne told the story of how he and his wife Rosemary built the house themselves, while they and their three children camped out in a small caravan in the grounds. One day the building inspector called by, took exception to the family having already moved in, having wrapped the frame around with polythene, and demanded that they leave. Colin Boyne asked him if that would

above: 'Kentlands', plan

be preferable, with the children continuing to camp out in such squalid conditions. He relented, work resumed, and in fact the inspector offered his own practical skills on weekends, so impressed was he with the project.

The construction is straightforward, and further simplified so that it ingeniously allowed non-experts with rudimentary craft skills to build it. The superstructure is formed of a timber frame, with main floor and ceiling joists running parallel to the main entrance axis (i.e. north-south), forming a grid of consistent 2.44m (8ft) bays across the house. The joists are twinned, with a gap between allowing the beams to 'grip' the vertical posts of the frame. The construction technique, and its consequent articulation, predate more well-known exponents of self-building, such as Walter Segal's 'Little House' in Highgate of 1964, the progenitor of his 1970s self-build housing schemes in Lewisham, and Ted Cullinan's own house in Camden, London, also of 1964.

Notes

1   Reyner Banham, *Guide to Modern Architecture*, London: Architectural Press, 1962.

2   Gordon Cullen, Townscape, London: Architectural Press, 1961. J. M.Richards, *The Functional Tradition in Early Industrial Buildings*, London: Architectural Press, 1958 (with photographs by Eric de Maré).

3   Ian Nairn, *Nairn's London*, Harmondsworth: Penguin, 1966, pp.164–5.

4   Gregory Dix, *The Shape of the Liturgy*, London: Dacre Press, 1943.

5   Keith Murray, 'Concern for the craft', *Architectural Review*, October 1976, p.205.

6   Edward Mills, *The Modern Church*, London: Architectural Press, 1956.

7   Robert Maguire in an email to the author, 25 June 2011.

8   Reyner Banham, *The New Brutalism: Ethic or Aesthetic?*, London: Architectural Press, 1966.

9   Maxwell Fry, *Horizon*, May 1946, cited in Bryan Appleyard, *The Pleasures of Peace: art and imagination in post-war Britain*, London: Faber and Faber, 1989.

10 Alison and Peter Smithson, *Architectural Design*, January 1955, p.1.

11 Robert Maguire, 'Anglican Church in Stepney', *Churchbuilding*, October 1962, p.18.

12 ibid., p.16.

13 For a discussion of Maguire & Murray's appropriation of the aedicule in churches, see Gerald Adler, 'Little Boxes' in *Scale: imagination, perception and practice in architecture*, Gerald Adler, Timothy Brittain-Catlin and Gordana Fontana-Giusti, (eds), Abingdon: Routledge, 2012.

14 Reyner Banham, 'A modern church on liturgical principles', *Architectural Review*, December 1960, p.400.

15 An anecdote recounted to the author by Robert Maguire.

16 Rudolf Wittkower, *Architectural Principles in the Age of Humanism*, London: Warburg Institute, 1949. For a discussion of Maguire's appropriation of idealist sources linked to Renaissance studies in architecture, see Elain Harwood, 'Liturgy and Architecture: The Development of the Centralised Eucharistic Space' in *The Twentieth Century Church, Twentieth Century Architecture 3, The Journal of the Twentieth Century Society* (1998), pp.49–74.

17 Robert Maguire, 'Meaning and Understanding' in *Towards a Church Architecture*, Peter Hammond, (ed.), London: The Architectural Press, 1962, p.69.

18 Peter Hammond (ed.), *Towards a Church Architecture*, London: The Architectural Press, 1962, p.142.

19 See Wolfgang Pehnt, *Rudolf Schwarz (1897–1961): Architekt einer anderen Moderne*, Stuttgart: Hatje, 1997.

20 For Senn's work, see Peter Hammond (ed.), *Towards a Church Architecture*, London: The Architectural Press, 1962 and Peter Hammond, *Liturgy and Architecture*, London: Barrie and Rockcliff, 1960.

21 Robert Maguire, 'Something out of the ordinary?' in *Architecture: Opportunities, Achievements. A report of the annual conference of the Royal Institute of British Architects held at the University of Hull, 14–17 July 1976*, Barbara Goldstein, (ed.), London: RIBA Publications, 1977, p.70.

22 See Gerald Adler, 'Something out of the 'Ordinary'' in *The Cultural Role of Architecture*, Paul Emmons, John Hendrix, Jane Lomholt, (eds), Abingdon: Routledge, 2012 (on which this account of the church at Bow Common is based).

23 John Eastwick-Field and John Stillman, *The Design and Practice of Joinery*, London: Architectural Press, 1958.

2 House

There has been a war and people have seen so many houses reduced to rubble that they no longer feel safe in their own homes which once seemed so quiet and secure. This is something that is incurable and will never be cured no matter how many years go by. True, we have a lamp on the table again, and a little vase of flowers, and pictures of our loved ones, but we can no longer trust any of these things because once, suddenly, we had to leave them behind, or because we have searched through the rubble for them in vain.[1]
Natalia Ginzburg, 'The Son of Man', *The Little Virtues*, 1962.

Although Maguire & Murray designed very few individual houses, it was the idea of the house, the smallest architectural unit in which human communities come together and live in close proximity, on which they drew in subsequent years. A handful of houses, mainly vicarages, were designed in the 1960s, following on from Maguire's house for the Boynes, but the practice's real architectural invention lay with rethinking communal housing, particularly for university students. Housing was far more than a theoretical and abstract concern of both men: they had personal experience of exploring alternatives in the 'Fabyc' community in which both lived from 1963.

Michael Murray's house at 6 Regent Square, Bloomsbury, London, once the studio of the artist Graham Sutherland, became the office of Maguire and Murray's practice from 1959 to 1964. At the AA, Maguire befriended an ex-student, Joseph Rykwert, later a distinguished writer on architecture, with whom he made common cause on matters of liturgical reform from a Catholic perspective. In 1953 he met Catherine Ginsberg, a charismatic Christian emigrée from pre-war Nazi Germany who practised existential psychotherapy. Ginsberg worshipped at Westminster Cathedral and her clients included many *Kindertransport* Jews from the Continent, as well as Jewish converts to Roman Catholicism and a group coalesced around her, forming a residential community in Rosary Gardens, near Gloucester Road, South Kensington. Maguire was part of this circle, and his first wife Robina, one of Colin Boyne's secretaries at the Architectural Press, joined him in the community when they married. In 1961, Keith Murray married Susan Harrison, whom he met through the Eastern Churches Circle, and in 1963 they joined the community when it moved to Kew.

opposite: **Stag Hill Court, University of Surrey, student housing**

Housing the Fabyc community

The move to Kew came after the nascent community began to grow, with new individuals and couples joining. Soon the house in South Kensington proved to be too small, and the community started to disperse, finding flats and houses over west and southwest London. The one constant was the regular Monday evening meeting. The structure of the community evolved slowly; large flats were found housing two couples and their children, with both family groups sharing one kitchen/dining room. Although this arrangement worked for pairs of couples, it did not foster the community spirit as a whole, and so they sought to consolidate by finding accommodation sufficiently large to house them all together. The first task was to get them on a firm financial footing, and they formed the first cooperative housing association. The two architects in their midst, Maguire and his AA friend, Peter Whiteley, took it on themselves to identify groups of houses on the market ripe for conversion. They used to view possible houses on a Saturday morning, and have scheme drawings ready by Monday morning to show the building societies in their search for a mortgage. When in the early 1960s four sizeable Victorian villas came up for sale near Kew Gardens, the community bought them and they became Maguire and Murray's first housing project.

The community, by now a formalised housing association, styled itself Fabyc, standing for 'family by choice'. The idea was that you would have a wider family, but by choice, not birth. Thus there was established, in middle-class Kew Gardens, a version of a kibbutz. The four villas were carved up internally into flats and maisonettes of

above: **Fabyc House, rear view from communal garden**

different sizes to suit the ten 'family' groupings comprising eventually 37 adults and 28 children: 65 residents in total. The building work was completed in 1963 and the community members moved in. Children lived with their parents, but kitchen/dining rooms were shared between pairs of (nuclear) families. Architecturally, Maguire devised simple brick and slate roof connecting buildings behind the shared entrances to the flats and houses. The rear gardens were opened up, forming a generous shared space. The years spent living communally paved the way for the radical student housing project at Surrey, begun in 1967.

The modern vicarage

The priest's house at St Paul's, Bow Common is located on the north side of the garden behind the church, together with the church's brick peripheral wall and its protruding east chapel, and the sacristy and meeting room to the south (see p.21). It acts as a frame to the garden, enabling it to function as an external space for both priest and congregation. The brickwork is pale grey stretcher-bond sand-lime, in contrast to the richer purplish colour of the church itself. The house is mostly single-storey, a two-storey tower emerging above the dining room and study. Like the projecting brick stack at Kentlands, this creates a Wrightian arrangement of a massive chimney breast oriented north–south and a narrow staircase running east–west, parallel to the overall 'grain' of the house. In a mannerist flourish, the chimney stack sits astride brick piers which define the bottom of the staircase. The stair leads up to a look-out, a generous sitting room with full glazing onto the garden beneath. This glass crown, a play on the glass hat sitting on top of the massive church, has that pungent detailing of heavy timber structural mullions supporting a flat projecting roof, anticipating Ted Cullinan's house at Camden (1964), while the overall form resembles Alison and Peter Smithson's Upper Lawn Pavilion at Fonthill, Wiltshire (1958–62).

At All Saints Church, Crewe (1962–67) the vicarage again helps to define and frame the garden, but in this case the building is contiguous with the tall volume of the church hall (see p.86). This leads to a well-considered south (garden) elevation, where box-like dormer windows lighting the hall to the east balance the first-floor windows of the bedrooms next door to the west. The detailing of these dormers is trim and flush with the brickwork below and underscored by the line of the gutter. It recalls Maguire's observation of vernacular structures on his 1949 travelling scholarship tour around Britain, in which he learnt from the clear formal separation of different parts of the building, a characteristic also seen in the Fabyc houses in London of the same period.

Presented as part of a continuous building fabric, and united with the church beneath their common pitched roof, the house at Crewe clearly relates to this fascination with the everyday. Since the Vicar had a working-class parish he did not want the vicarage to stand out, and by sharing the same roof form and material, the monumental effect of the church is also modified.

top: All Saints church, Crewe, vicarage, hall and west side of church
above: St Joseph's church, Northolt, vicarage

The vicarage at St Joseph's, Northolt, West London (1966–70) is once again separate from its slightly monumental church. It provides an informal counterpart to the beautiful composition of church, baptistery and chapel, and stakes out the northern corner of the site, on the busy Yeading Lane, opposite the free-standing belfry. The house has a compact layout, with rooms aligned single-banked to one side of the stair hall, all giving onto the south-west garden and a view onto the gaunt, blank walls of the church (see p.95). In common with the church, the materials are grey concrete block with a roof of folded zinc. The aesthetic is mid-1960s industrial while retaining in scale and atmosphere a domestic feeling to the bedrooms and living spaces.

The house at the Church of the Ascension, Hulme, Manchester (1969–72) rounds off this series, playing an important role in the composition of the church on its site, framing the garden, and giving a modicum of private, external space to the priest and congregation (see p.99). The modest ground-floor living zone with a flow of space from entrance to kitchen has a generosity of outlook and scale which allows the incumbent to hold small meetings in the shadow of the church. Its simple, low-pitched zinc roofs inaugurate a fantastic geometry of roof planes to the church, becoming more compli-cated as they turn and rise, ziggurat-fashion, to the apex.

These vicarages suggest community with their nurturing garden spaces shared between the vicar's family and the church congregation. Internally, they usually had linear plans, with box-like private bedrooms juxtaposed against more open-plan living areas, resembling many architects' houses of mid-century, most notably those by the Danish architect Jørn Utzon. As homes for the clergy and their families the houses had to conform to well-defined patterns of domestic behaviour, whatever innovations were made in the churches adjoining them. When Maguire and Murray came to design student housing in the 1960s and 1970s, they had more scope for innovations that led to the now familiar typology of the student village.

Oxford: Trinity College and Blackwell's

In 1959, Robert Maguire was invited to design a substantial amount of accommodation, the bulk of it student residential sets, for Trinity College, Oxford, behind the shops on Broad Street and the college garden to the north. Sir Arthur Norrington, President of the College, initially sent a letter, out of the blue, to another Robert Maguire, an architect in Lancashire who, having realised he was not the Maguire in question, promptly forwarded the letter to the right place. The college insisted on having tradi-tional 'sets' of bedrooms combined with sitting rooms off staircases. It was a formula that had served Oxbridge well for centuries but Maguire and Murray, starting their formal partnership with this commission and the church at Perry Beeches, made some interesting variations on the theme.

The Cumberbatch buildings and quads, named after the College's benefactor for the works, comprise a sequence of residential sets and some teaching rooms, organised around a tight, enclosed quad behind the shops on Broad Street and a long quad opening up to the college lawns to the north. The long, parallel sides of the main quad are flanked by T. G. Jackson's Gothic Revival New Building of 1881–2 to the west and the War Memorial Library of 1925 to the east. Maguire and Murray's buildings plug the gaps at either end: a squat tower, attached to the north end of the library, partially closes the gap, framing views of the lush lawns in the garden beyond, while a four-storey range of building completely fills in the south side, a passageway to the east continuing through to the small quad. The tower, known as Cumberbatch North Building, avails itself of the half-storey difference in level between the quad and the garden below, rather in the manner of a Georgian terraced house, where a basement area gives directly onto the garden, replaced here by a lecture theatre beneath the entrance junction with the Library and three Fellows' rooms below the tower. A small flight of steps rises up to the Danson Room, a grand reception space. Above this sit three storeys of student sets, with protruding oak-framed window boxes held between bands of board-marked concrete, the upstands to the concrete slabs that sandwich the building. The tower is capped by a pyramidal roof in slate, whose broad expanse is cut into by a lower strip of gutter, set into the roof plane and thus preserving the outline of the form uninterrupted. A narrow range of clerestory glazing appears towards the top, with a final glass pyramid at the apex. This fragmentation has earned it the nickname 'the pagoda', although its resemblance to the classic seventeenth-century Japanese castle form, at Matsumoto and Himeji, would be nearer the mark. It is only when you examine the plans that you are aware of the powerful cruciform of U-shaped load-bearing walls (in blue engineering brick) balanced by the pinwheel planning of the Fellows' rooms, all of which bears a resemblance to the form and expression of Kiyonori Kikutake's (b.1928) Sky House, Tokyo (1958), crossed with the Japanese-inspired pinwheel plans of Frank Lloyd Wright as filtered through the house designs of Richard Neutra.

Cumberbatch South building (now called Kettelfield Hall) shares the aesthetic of the 'pagoda' opposite, but has quite a different organisation within. The ground and attic storeys comprise conventional two-room sets which sandwich a piano nobile of six duplex sets. These have sitting rooms overlooking the main quad to the north, lit by generous double-height windows, and have sleeping platforms to the south, with clerestory window strips giving onto the small quad beyond. Tucked beneath the sleeping mezzanines are the shower rooms and WCs. The architects are beginning to privilege the conviviality of sitting spaces over the intensely private realms of bed 'rooms' and to alter the hierarchical relationship between these two zones, a development that would find its full flowering in their later work at Guildford. What is apparent at Trinity is the struggle that Maguire and Murray were having with finding the appropriate expression of a building, and the resolution of conflicting scales between the front and back (or outside and inside) of a building. These questions of scale had already been broached in the church projects, where the vicarages sit in subservience to the churches. With Cumberbatch South, overlooking the garden quad, the architects make a convincing scale relationship by juxta-posing the tall proportions of the oriel windows at first-floor level. These are curiously

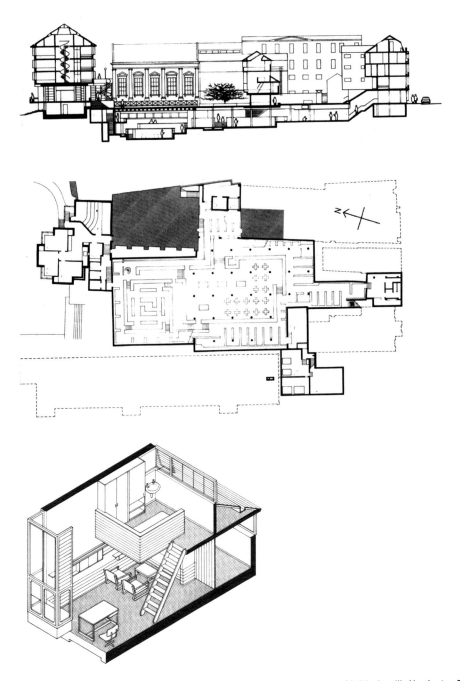

top: Trinity College, Oxford, section showing Cumberbatch quadrangles with Blackwell's Norrington Room
bookshop below
middle: Trinity College, Oxford, lower ground floor and Blackwell's Norrington Room basement bookshop
above: Trinity College, Oxford, duplex room in Cumberbatch South building

top: Trinity College, Oxford, Cumberbatch South building, north facade. This photo shows the decorative 'Cosmati' pavement and the screen wall masking Blackwell's bookshop
above: Trinity College, Oxford, Cumberbatch North building

top: Trinity College, Oxford, Cumberbatch North building
above left: Trinity College, Oxford, small quad and Cumberbatch South building
above right: Blackwell's bookshop, Norrington Room

off-centre in relation to the attic loggias above, and respond to the giant order of the adjacent library. The architectural language is perhaps more convincing on the 'domestic' rear side, overlooking the small enclosed quad to the south, with its articulated walls and little slated pent roofs.

The main quad (the 'Library Quad') has a very pleasing textured stone floor, even though Nicholas Taylor disparaged it in the *Architectural Review* as 'an irritating neo-Roman mosaic in a kind of Cosmati pebble-work'.[2] It is underneath this floor that Maguire and Murray's ingenuity in planning can be discovered. They encouraged Trinity to negotiate with their neighbour to the south-east, Blackwell's bookshop, and strike a mutually beneficial deal. Trinity benefitted from rental income on (or rather under) its land, Blackwell's got 4 km (2½ miles) of book-shelving and a far more rational layout, and the architects landed an extra commission. Most significantly, architecture as a whole was given an exemplar of sensitive and satisfying comprehensive redevelopment of urban infill. The section describes the street-level entrance on Broad Street, then the descent down a straight flight of steps at the back of the original shop. Ahead is a subterranean cavern of books, the Norrington Room (named after the President of Trinity), a vista of descending floor planes culminating in the square pit of the philosophy and divinity sections. All this happens beneath a specular louvred ceiling, concealing fluorescent lighting above. This suspended ceiling is omitted from the ceiling of 'the pit', where a coffered ceiling is revealed. (The specular louvred ceiling has been replaced later, in one of the usual shop re-fits, by something more brash.) The dons would be surprised to learn that these elegant circular coffers are in fact concrete manhole rings, testimony to Robert Maguire's stint at the *Architects' Journal* in the late 1950s, where he nurtured an encyclopaedic knowledge of building materials and components.

Stag Hill Court, University of Surrey

After their first Oxford building, the practice enjoyed a commission with few constraints. A contact of Peter Whiteley's was instrumental in introducing the partners to their next client, and in 1967 Maguire and Murray were commissioned by the University of Surrey to design student residential accommodation on their campus just outside the centre of Guildford, in the shadow of the simplified Gothic Revival cathedral, recently completed after a 30-year building campaign to the designs of Sir Edward Maufe (1883–1974). Here, on a prominent site some distance from the city centre, we can experience a panorama of twentieth-century British architectural history, from the revivalism of the cathedral, to the technocratic, gridded masterplan by George Grenfell-Baines of Building Design Partnership (BDP), redolent of Harold Wilson's appeal to forge a new Britain in the 'white heat of the technological revolution'. Maguire and Murray's work, described on completion as 'possibly one of the most important and successful statements of its kind for two decades', adds to the mixture.[3]

The south-east facing site, some 1.1 hectares (2¾ acres), was on a hillside of clay prone to slippage. The task was to house at least 400 students to University Grants Committee (UGC) cost limits. Here, at last, Maguire and Murray were able to apply their experience of communal living gained at Fabyc, in a scheme that exceeded in scope anything the practice had yet seen. They were fortunate in having an enlightened client who allowed them a six-month research period to really get under the skin of their students and expand the brief as they always tried to do. The University was having to contend with excessive rates of drop-out and suicides, and the architects asked a series of penetrating questions, to which only honest answers were accepted. It was akin to their experience of existential psychotherapy, of getting to the heart of the matter when designing Fabyc House.

The students at Surrey were quite different from those at Oxford. The University had been created from Battersea College of Technology and relocated to Guildford as a consequence of the Robbins report of 1963, which recommended that all such establishments become upgraded to universities. Maguire and Murray's research discovered that many of the students were unprepared for student life and not particularly gregarious. Decamped from inner London to the hills of Surrey, they were often the first generation of their families to have gone on to tertiary education, and frequently felt isolated. One of the ideas that the practice promoted was to 'try to get the brief formulated in terms of needs rather than of "solution-images"'.[4] They were explicitly resisting the findings of the Niblett Committee of 1957 which favoured halls of residence as the best form of contemporary student housing. What they developed was a series of diagrams exploring the ideal hierarchies which should obtain in groups of people living together, predicated on an optimum group size of ten students per 'house'. The concept of the house unit was apparent in a series of terraces running down the slope of the hill, looking like a version of working-class housing in a northern town crossed with the serendipity of a Tuscan hilltop village. The ideal number of ten students living together, behind the front door of their house, was 'not ... so low that a clique might be formed which would exclude one or two students ... and not so high that any one student would feel himself unable to speak up over any unpleasant matter.'[5] There were also practical considerations, such as the optimum number of people using a shared kitchen. While the organising principles were illustrated by a series of diagrams reminiscent of Christopher Alexander's patterns in *Notes on the Synthesis of Form* (1964), the footprint of the terraces was staggered in order to maintain an unbroken roof plane covering all the houses. At the front, the roofs swooped down to the height of a person, with clipped eaves. At the apex of the roofs, instead of a conventional ridge, the roofs were topped by a short section of flat roof. The decision to flatten the ridge in this way was a result of the Planning Committee saying that the initial designs were not 'cubistic enough'.[6]

The rather startling external appearance of the houses meant that the internal planning was overlooked, at least by the general public. Had they ventured inside, they would have found a pair of staggered house forms joined together to form each house, with three internal doors on the ground floor, each giving onto a shared lobby, wardrobes

top: Stag Hill Court, Surrey University, Guildford, site plan
above: Stag Hill Court, 'rules' governing offsets: adjacent houses are always linked by a shared roof plane

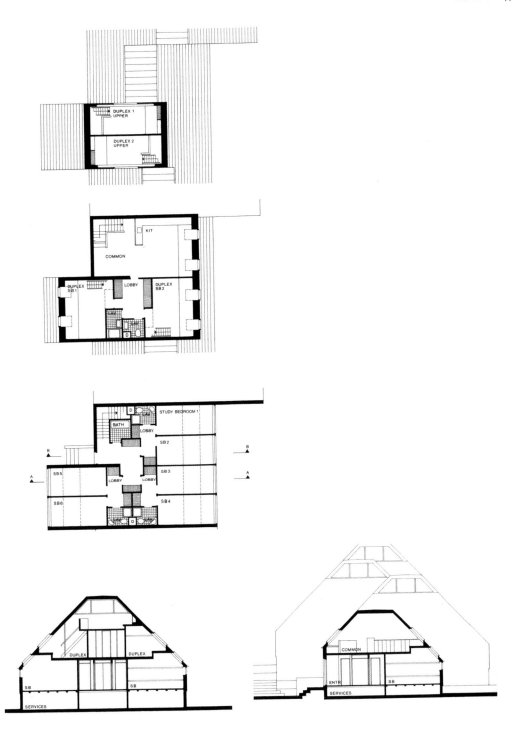

above: Stag Hill Court, standard 10-person house, plans and sections

top: Stag Hill Court
above: Stag Hill Court, shared duplex study-bedroom

and shower-room/WC shared between two study-bedrooms – six students, then, on the ground floor. Upstairs, winding round the only bathroom in the house (now redundant as students today eschew baths for the convenience of showers), you come directly into a large kitchen and common room, with a door that gives onto another shared lobby serving four more students. These rooms, however, differ from the others in that they have narrow internal staircases going up to large sleeping platforms. What we have in the case of these attic rooms with mezzanine floors is the Trinity duplex revisited, but at Surrey two students were accommodated, each with his or her personal space on each level. Ten students in all were thus sandwiched around the communal hub. The site plan replicates the hierarchy of the interiors on a greater scale, with a large central space in the centre of the whole ensemble, half-way down the slope of the hill and an intricate spider's web of ginnels and alleyways connecting the terraces. It is a version of the kind of densely joined-up housing in continental Europe, known as 'mat design' in some European avant-garde circles, such as *Siedlung Halen*, Bern (1955–61) by Atelier 5, and numerous schemes by Giancarlo de Carlo in Italy. As with the Trinity scheme, Stag Hill was innovative in terms of construction. To deal with the very difficult site conditions the whole scheme sits on a stepped concrete raft, a giant 'snowshoe' spreading over the site, which distributed the load evenly. To this day Stag Hill is the most popular student accommodation at Surrey, and where the best parties happen.

Bramcote: boxes without tricks

The student and staff accommodation for the Anglican seminary at Bramcote, a village just outside Nottingham, continued the thinking about individual and group living initiated at Stag Hill. St John's Theological College, a constituent part of the University of Nottingham, was similar in its genesis to the University of Surrey. If Stag Hill resulted in a picturesque layout, albeit one originating from a strict and dense array of parallel blocks, then Bramcote reverted to the more conventional plan arrangement of short blocks defining courtyard-like spaces. Formerly the London College of Divinity, Bramcote accorded with the Church of England's policy of linking seminaries with universities: St John's degrees would henceforth be awarded by Nottingham. The beautiful site was centred on The Grove, an early Victorian house set in its mature garden. The oval of lawn fringed by mature trees was sacrosanct, and new building, accommodating some 80 students and staff, including married couples, with chapel, dining room, teaching and other social spaces was restricted to the area around the old house. The Grove, a four-square villa of the 1830s, is the formal point of arrival. It is 'framed' by two long parallel blocks running south-east to north-west comprising the single-students' residences (study-bedrooms off a double-banked corridor) and the social block. A smaller entrance courtyard to The Grove is defined by another, shorter, block housing the caretaker and boiler room. The two long blocks then link to the old house by means of covered loggias, imparting a cloister atmosphere to the ensemble. Beyond the single-students' block, located mid-way between the boundary road to the north-west and the protected lawn to the south-east, is the block of married-students' flats, the only building in the scheme to run normal to the prevailing grain of new buildings. This serves to break up the open space, forming two landscaped courtyards between the furthest-flung terraces of staff houses on the north-east boundary.

At Guildford, the mathematical array of housing is countered by the picturesque effects wrought by the sloping site, as well as by the L-shaped paired 'houses' forming well-scaled subgroupings. Bramcote's less pronounced slope means that compositional variations provide the visual relief. The block of married-students' flats, for example, has its north-east terminated by an extra storey, forming a tower-like punctuation mark at the constriction between the two furthest landscape courts and the three fingers of staff and student accommodation. This device resembles the way the Cumberbatch 'pagoda' controls the transition from quad to garden at Trinity, or the way the campanile forms the fulcrum between the piazza and piazzetta in Venice, with the backdrop of St Mark's and the Doge's Palace. In terms of detail, it is achieved quietly but fastidiously, with the use of unadorned materials and components. The scheme was praised by the reviewer for the *Architects' Journal* as a 'Box without tricks' whose 'stringent simplicity suggests a constrained brief, a low budget and a compressed timescale; gone are the bravura sections of Guildford, the intellectualism of Bow, and the profound sense of structure of Trinity ...; instead the exercise is a skilful distillation of the good that is in placid

above: 'Venice', Robert Maguire, 1951. The *Serenissima's* picturesque effects, allied with a consistent architectural language based on a common pallete of materials and repeated window-types, would characterise the architecture of Bramcote

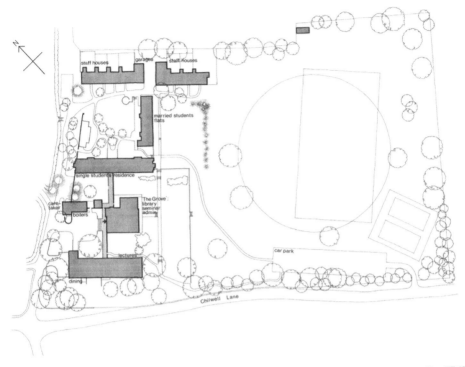

top: St John's College, Bramcote, near Nottingham, site plan
above: St John's College, view of staff houses from the west

grey concrete masonry blocks, stained softwood, asbestos tiles, flag pavings and grass.'[7] The unsung concrete block would characterise some of the best (and some of the most mediocre) of British architecture in the 1970s but when used judiciously and carefully, with utmost attention to junctions, corners and openings, as was the case at Bramcote, it managed to contribute to a 'poetry of the everyday'. Maguire and Murray managed to conjure up 'something out of the ordinary' with a 'concern for the craft' in schemes such as St John's, as well as in the subsequent housing projects through the 1970s.[8] This poetry of the everyday was enacted through a thorough knowledge and command of building trades. The fair-faced concrete blocks, for instance, are deployed to minimise cuts and bodges; the roofs, in asbestos-cement slates, are simple double-pitches, avoiding unsightly – and costly – hipped junctions. All this speaks of Maguire's rigour in using rational building techniques, harking back to his student reading of the 'truth to materials' doctrine of Frank Lloyd Wright, combined with his promotion of Danish housing while at the *Architects' Journal* in the late 1950s, plus working on the illustrations for the Stillman and Eastwick-Field book on joinery and subsequently writing the ironmongery pages for *Specification*. Murray, too, cared about the way objects were fashioned: his own background as a craftsman made him immune from being a 'paper' designer.

North Oxford *Existenzminimum*

Cumberbatch was conceived in the early 1960s, an age of fantastic opulence by contrast with what came afterwards. By the mid-1970s, the world of publicly-funded building had changed. Even more than Bramcote, the nine married students' houses designed for St Stephen's House, a theological college of the Church of England at Oxford, exhibit the Bauhaus attribute of *Existenzminimum* at its most extreme. The site at Norham Gardens, north Oxford, is the back garden of a large Victorian house, 650m² in area.[9] Along its perimeter is shoehorned a row of six houses on the north-eastern edge, and three at the end. The houses are tiny: some 32m², with a combined kitchen/dining/sitting area on the ground floor, and a study-bedroom with walk-in shower/WC upstairs. As at Stag Hill, the bedroom is cut into the steeply pitched roof-space. To comply with fire regulations there is an escape hatch from the bedroom should the staircase, open to the kitchen-cum-living area below, become smoke-filled. It works as housing because the couples do not imagine that they will be here for life: stays are reckoned not to exceed two years. As students, they can also use other university facilities, and do not depend solely on their houses for study and socialising. What Maguire and Murray demonstrated was that through painstaking and intelligent design on a minimum budget, a common building type such as the house could be re-imagined. They showed that good buildings could be achieved by creative design, at space standards *below* those of Parker Morris, or by eschewing solutions approved by the Building Regulations. The houses work because they are conceived volumetrically, so that the study area at the end of the first floor bedroom is located above the flipped-up ceiling to the garden front of the living area. The planning means that the 'front' doors are on the outer edge, down a ginnel covered by the roof overhang. The 'back' doors giving onto the secluded, shared garden have increased privacy, and greater scale, due to their more open, glazed facades and generosity of section offered by the cranked ceiling. One critic thought there was much more here than met the eye: 'At first sight this tiny scheme would appear to be little more than a sensitive, low-key, low-cost means of providing a few additional square metres of floor space. One's second reaction might be to draw comparisons between this and the more elaborate architectural statements which have frequently been adopted by Oxbridge colleges in recent years.'[10]

above: St Stephen's House, Oxford, married students' houses, plan and section

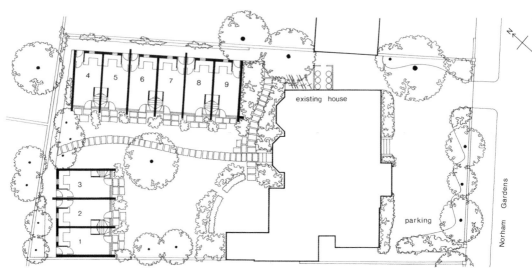

top: St Stephen's House, houses framing communal garden
above: St Stephen's House, married students' houses, site plan

Sussex terraces

The modest scheme for St Stephen's House was followed by two far more visible
schemes in the 1970s. When Maguire and Murray were commissioned by the University
of Sussex, they responded with similar modesty, at odds with the expansive panache
of the early campus buildings by Sir Basil Spence. Sussex was the most radical of
university campuses in the late 1960s. A group of students visited Stag Hill Court
and, following a rent strike, the Estates Department acceded to the Student Union's
request for Maguire and Murray to be appointed as architects in 1971. Their collaborative approach was seen by Sussex as a conciliatory move; commissioning a practice
like theirs would, it was hoped, show the university authorities in a good light. The site
was a hillside similar to that at Guildford, but this time single-storey stepped-section
terraced houses were developed, running along the contours, with the unglamorous but
apt name of East Slope. Rather than resembling family houses like Stag Hill, the Sussex
terraces had a stepped section, comprising low-lying, flat-roofed single-storey apartments. They hugged the hillside, much in the manner of Atelier 5's work in Switzerland.
The scheme had an ingenious, highly economical plan. Lanes ran east–west up the

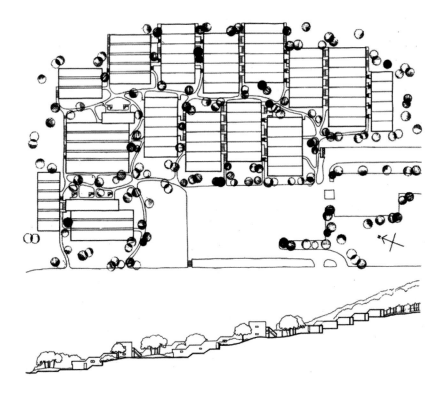

above: **East slope student flats, University of Sussex, Falmer, site plan and section**

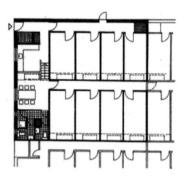

top: East slope student flats, model of study bedroom
top right: Section, and plan of a flat
above: Rooftop view

slope. With suggestions of Montmartre, the pathways from which the flats were entered were stepped with 'landings' formed and marked by trees. Internally, they were organised on two half-levels, running down the site contours, with one single-banked corridor giving access to four study-bedrooms at the higher level, then with this pattern repeated at the lower level, down a short internal stair. This is located in the entrance zone, containing an upper-level kitchen, and lower-level dining and bathroom/WC area. The study-bedrooms are lit by rooflights, with a built-in desk looking out to the west, through a mansard type window at eye-level. You look out over the flat roof of your friends off the corridor below. The overall massing is not dissimilar to Denys Lasdun's student terraces at the University of East Anglia, Norwich (1964–68), and its continental, Mediterranean holiday character was underlined by the headline in Brighton's *Evening Argus*, 'Costa del Campus is booming', in reaction to the successful holiday-lets scheme run by the University during the long summer vacations.[11]

Bloomsbury mix

The practice had no significant project in central London before 1974, when they were commissioned by the Lutheran Council of Great Britain to design their international student centre, with associated church, in the densely built streets of the former Skinners' Company estate in Bloomsbury. A decade earlier they had built a Lutheran church at Harlow and now had the opportunity to work to a multifaceted brief involving urban infill, a typical feature of 1970s architecture in reaction against the comprehensive redevelopment typical of the previous decade.

The International Lutheran Student Centre (1975–78) was an important project for Maguire & Murray as it sought to establish comfortable student housing within the confines of a stretch of 'estate' London, originally Georgian, but subsequently overlain with Victorian and twentieth-century rebuilding and at that time in a neglected condition. The scheme represents perhaps the practice's most urban project, incorporating a basement church (see p.92) with the same qualities as their existing work in this field. The site stretches between Sandwich Street in the west to Thanet Street in the east, where the striped brick Thanet Street New Schools by the architects Milford, Teulon and Cronk had interrupted the terraced housing in 1872.

The two street elevations are similar, comprising six bays of oriel windows, some of which extend virtually to the ground, and capped by a continuous glazed attic storey. Connecting the two blocks are link buildings containing the dining room and chaplaincy, which give onto a delightful secret courtyard garden. The study-bedrooms are reached on both sides of internal corridors, with half the rooms facing the streets, and half looking onto the internal courtyard. A main staircase and a secondary one for escape lie at either end of the corridor.

Although the ground floor is at the same level as the street outside, the actual ground level represented by the garden is half a storey lower, as was typical for Georgian houses such as would originally have stood on the site. The church is located in the

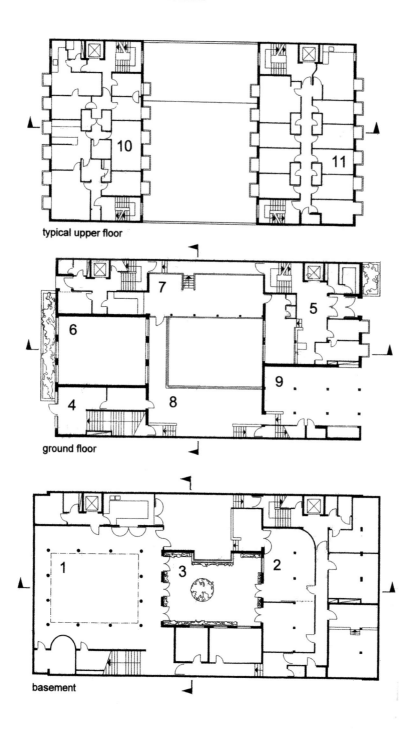

typical upper floor

ground floor

basement

top: Lutheran Centre, Bloomsbury, London, plans

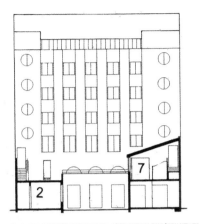

The Lutheran Centre

KEY

basement

1   church
2   chaplaincy
3   courtyard

ground floor

4   church entrance
5   hostel/ chaplaincy entrance
6   upper part of church
7   breakfast room
8   terrace
9   staff parking

upper floors

10   student flats
11   study bedrooms

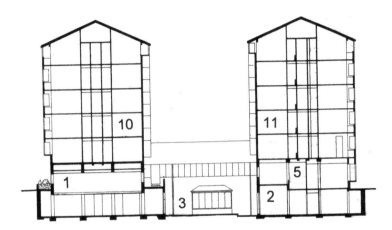

basement of Sandwich Street, but so arranged that its row of high-level semicircular 'thermal' windows are at ground level on Sandwich Street, but owing to the drop down to the garden level behind, there is enough height for three full-length glazed doors to the courtyard – a reprise of the clever sectional design seen at Trinity Cumberbatch.

The whole project is a well-judged design that satisfies the users (the oriels turn out to provide study carrels for each study-bedroom), the aims of the Lutheran church, and the building's urban location. The elevations are well modulated and have a good scale relationship with the diverse surrounding fabric, while at the same time mediating between the scale of the institution as a whole, and the expression of the individual. If the church interior (see p.92) reminds one of Frank Lloyd Wright, then the facade

top: Lutheran Centre, north-south section looking west
above: Lutheran Centre, east-west cross-section looking north

composition echoes the aesthetic of the English Arts and Crafts movement, something that AA students of Maguire's generation were familiar with from the teaching of John Brandon-Jones who championed Philip Webb, W. R. Lethaby and C. F. A. Voysey. The planarity of the brown garden-wall bond brickwork (above ground floor level), canti-levered window-box slabs and timber window frames is very much of its time. It is a credit to the client that the building is so well maintained. The cedar window frames are regularly oiled to keep their original tone, which would be ruined by staining or painting.

above: Lutheran Centre, facade to Thanet Street (hostel entrance)
opposite: Lutheran Centre, courtyard facade

More houses

In the 1990s, Robert Maguire's new practice, Maguire & Co, founded after Keith Murray's retirement from the practice in 1988, attracted a good deal of work in the Middle East, including a house for Abdul Aziz Modiamigh in Riyadh, Saudi Arabia, unfortunately never executed owing to the first Gulf war (1990–91). It offered Maguire the chance to combine his early Modernist, even Purist, interests with the inward looking, cloistered cubic massing of the regional vernacular. From his stay with the Nicholsons in Cumberland, Maguire remembered Leslie Martin's Brackenfell, near Brampton (1934–9), a modern brick house built for the textile manufacturer and artist Alistair Morton, and also the Arts and Crafts interiors of Winifred Nicholson's family house nearby.

Among the commissions from Oxford Colleges of these later years, Hazel Court for Jesus College (1988–92), ten student houses of four students each grouped around a U-shaped courtyard, is an object lesson in economical planning – a sophisticated take on the banality of received forms and materials, and a creative interpretation of the client's and users' needs. So far, so normal. Yet Maguire managed to transform this humdrum, everyday type into something rather special. The courtyard pushes the houses out to the site edge (would students really relish back gardens?) forming a semi-private entrance court, 'guarded' by the laundry pavilion. This is common ground for all residents. Then the houses are tightly – if conventionally – organised around winding staircases with large study-bedrooms looking either out over the suburban allotment gardens, or into the courtyard. It is the attic storey which surprises and delights. Here, in the best position in the building, is the house kitchen-cum-sitting-room, a shared space open to all. On the outside it has a dormer window making a chunky composition with a bold brick chimney-breast (hiding soil/vent pipes). On the inside courtyard

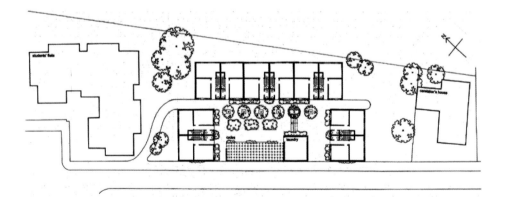

above: Student houses, Hazel Court for Jesus College, Oxford, ground and site plan
opposite: Hazel Court

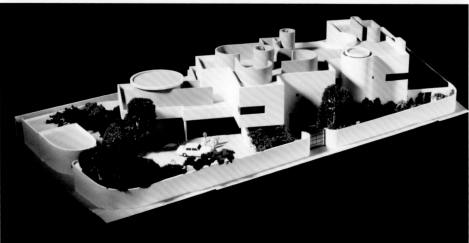

elevation there is a continuous run of windows extending to the full width of the house with their heads touching the eaves of the roof – a reprise of the clerestory detail at the Lutheran Centre which serves to lighten the roof visually.

top: Hazel Court, rear view across allotment gardens
above: House for Mr Abdul Aziz Modiamigh, Riyadh, model

Rethinking the rural house

This chapter ends with the house that Maguire designed for his own retirement. Located in Ettrickbridge, near Selkirk in the Scottish Borders, it is a three-generation house called Hopewater. Maguire had always questioned the sociological basis of our living conditions, and his answer takes the form of two apartments conjoined. At one end is the apartment for his stepson and his young family, at the opposite end live Maguire and his architectural historian wife Alison, whose researches into seventeenth-century house planning revealed 'apartment living' as a governing principle. From the outside it is quite inconspicuous, with a long slated double-pitched roof

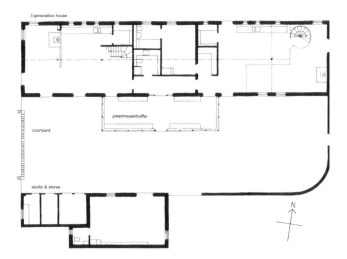

top: Hopewater House, Ettrickbridge, ground floor plan
above: Hopewater House, view from village street

above: **Hopewater House, living hall**

sprinkled with black-framed dormer windows, each with its own pitched roof half-engaged with the white rendered wall beneath. Inside at the 'grandparents' end, the centrally located bedroom gives onto a mezzanine floor ending in a spiral staircase that rises up through the living room positioned at the end of the house. Even in this precious location, the box contains a final trick, as we experience a great release of space in this brilliantly lit living hall: a medieval solar redux.[12]

Notes

1   Natalia Ginzburg, 'The Son of Man' in *The Little Virtues*, Manchester: Carcanet, 1985, p.49, trans. Dick Davis. Originally published in *Le piccole virtù*, Turin: Einadi, 1962.
2   Nicholas Taylor, 'Historic Patterns', *Architectural Review*, November 1966, p.339.
3   Corin Hughes Stanton, 'Freedom in court', *Design*, September 1971, p.46.
4   Robert Maguire, 'Nearness to need', *RIBA Journal*, April 1971, Architects' approach to architecture.
5   ibid., p.145.
6   'The Borough turns down University's Staghill Plan', *Surrey Advertiser & County Times*, 30 September 1967.
7   Terry Bestwick, 'Box without tricks', *Architects' Journal*, 20 October 1971, pp.846–7.
8   See Robert Maguire, 'Something out of the ordinary?' in *Architecture: Opportunities, Achievements. A report of the annual conference of the Royal Institute of British Architects held at the University of Hull, 14–17 July 1976*, Barbara Goldstein, (ed.), London: RIBA Publications, 1977. The lecture by Maguire at the conference was reprinted by the *Architects' Journal* with a completely different (and misleading) title: 'The value of tradition', *Architects' Journal*, 18 August 1976, pp.292–5. See also Keith Murray, 'Concern for the craft', *Architectural Review*, October 1976, pp.204–6.
9   Job architects at Norham Gardens were Alan Berman and Charles Brackenbury.
10 Dean Hawkes, 'Space standards and St Stephen's House' in 'Building Study: Housing for married students at St Stephen's House, Oxford', *Architects' Journal*, 25 January 1978, pp.159–70.
11 *Evening Argus*, 9 September 1976, p.12.
12 The reference to the solar recalls the fact that Maguire's second wife Alison is an architectural historian. She collaborated with Andor Gomme to write *Design and Planning the Country House: from castle donjons to Palladian boxes*, London and New Haven: Yale University Press, 2008.

3   Church

A serious house on serious earth it is,
In whose blent air all our compulsions meet,
Are recognised, and robed as destinies.
                    Philip Larkin, 'Church Going', *The Less Deceived*, 1955.

The church, as building type and institution, was the rock on which Robert Maguire and Keith Murray founded their partnership. The Church of England, and subsequently other Christian denominations, were faithful clients of the practice. Six new church buildings span the 1960s; taken together, they demonstrate the maturing art of Maguire and Murray and the development of their architectural craft and testify to the changing architectural sensibilities undergone by the practice during this decade. They are evidence that the motto from W. R. Lethaby, 'nearness to need', adopted by the practice was an apt phrasing for their architecture of economy and appropriate symbolic content. There were other kinds of commission and other building types during this period, several of which form ensembles with these churches, such as the residential accommodation at St Mary's Abbey, and the various vicarages.

Soon after Maguire received the commission for St Paul's, Bow Common, he received a letter from Peter Hammond, who became the driving force behind liturgical reform in the Church of England, and a firm believer in the need for the design of churches to reflect contemporary approaches to ritual. He had seen Edward Mills's book *The Modern Church*, published in 1956, and wanted to know more about Maguire's hypothetical project which Mills had included. Hammond was planning to write a book on the modern renaissance of religious art when he met Maguire and Keith Murray in Café Torino, Soho, one of the chief haunts of bohemian London, much frequented by architects and artists.

Liturgical reform
Like Murray, Hammond had a deep and abiding interest in Eastern Orthodoxy, having been behind the translation of Vladimir Lossky's influential *Essai sur la Théologie Mystique de l'Eglise d'Orient*, first published in Paris in 1944. After a distinguished war

opposite: St Matthew's Church, Perry Beeches, Birmingham

record followed by reading history at Oxford he was ordained as a priest in the Church of England; in his church at Bagendon in the Cotswolds he celebrated Mass standing behind the altar and facing the congregation: revolutionary at the time. This meeting of like minds encouraged Hammond to write *Liturgy and Architecture*, his major book published in 1961, instead of his previous project. In 1957, he founded the New Churches Research Group jointly with Maguire and Murray, to which Susan Murray eventually became secretary. Britain came late to reform of the liturgy; as a movement it had its origins in interwar continental Europe, particularly in Belgium, Italy and France. Germany was where the most interesting architectural implications of a renewed liturgy were played out, particularly in the great Roman Catholic churches of Rudolf Schwarz and Dominikus Böhm. According to Hammond,

> *The church is seen first and foremost as the place where the local Christian community gathers for the eucharist. This is its essential function, to which everything else is subordinate. The liturgy itself is regarded not as something performed by the clergy alone, but as a corporate action in which everyone has an active part to play. Hence the current [1958] experiments with novel types of church plan based on the square, the circle, the ellipse and the trapezoid. Such plans are not primarily the result of the freedom conferred by modern methods of construction. They are the outcome of the Church's new understanding of itself, and of the liturgy in which its essential character should be most fully realized and made manifest.*[1]

The New Churches Research Group began organising conferences where clergy and architects could discuss the effects of liturgical reform on church design. At one such event in early 1959 Peter Vowles, vicar of Perry Beeches, Birmingham, asked if Maguire would design his new church. Shortly after this he was asked by Sir Arthur Norrington, President of Trinity College, Oxford, to be the architect for the Cumberbatch project. Thus it dawned on Maguire, then still working at the Architectural Press, that in order to take on these jobs he would need a more formal architectural practice with the normal support of an office. He asked Austin Winkley, an ex-student of the AA whom he had tutored in his final year, to come into partnership with him, but Winkley, who went on to design a number of Roman Catholic churches which show the clear debt to Maguire's architectural thinking about liturgical reform, had set his sights elsewhere. Murray meanwhile was Managing Director of Watts & Co., in addition to running the Artist's Management Association which looked after artists' and craftsmen's paperwork. It occurred to Maguire that his friend might make an excellent practice partner, for despite Murray's lack of knowledge in architectural design and building construction, he knew how to run a design business, and understood money, clients and contracts. Maguire had actually been using an upstairs room at Watts & Co, at 10 Dacre Street, Westminster, as his office since 1958; and so the partnership of Robert Maguire & Keith Murray was born in October 1959.

Faced with the choice between equal partnership in a burgeoning architectural practice, and his position at Watts, Murray decided to throw in his lot with Maguire. He was already committed to designing the mosaics for St Paul's, Bow Common, and had done preliminary designs, and contacted the firm of Melloni and Moretti in Murano for samples and colours. The mosaics could not be started until the church was complete and, in order to give his time to the architectural practice, Murray proposed the painter Charles Lutyens, a mutual friend of both Murray's and Maguire's (and a Fabyc member), for the task. The conflicting roles of designer-craftsman and designer-architect proved difficult for Murray to reconcile. While committed to the latter, he came to suffer feelings of inferiority towards Maguire, which contributed to antagonism between the two in later years and led eventually to the breakup of the partnership.

Since St Paul's was nearing completion, it was adopted by the newly-forged practice as its first building, and is normally credited as being by both partners, although the architecture and the furniture were purely Maguire's. The six churches that follow were the joint work of both men, assisted by project architects, and are testimony to the intensely collaborative relationship between the two.

Perry Beeches

The romantic-sounding Perry Beeches where Peter Vowles's parish was located is actually a northern suburb of Birmingham, a place of semi-detached houses dating from the interwar years. The population continued to expand in the 1960s, still at a very low density, with acres of grass – as verges, in front gardens and in the centre of the roundabout just to the south of the church site. Vowles and his congregation knew they wanted a church based on modern liturgical principles; they not only got this, but also got a thoroughly modern aesthetic as well. An interwar parish hall was to be retained, and this formed the north-west side of an intimate courtyard. The church itself was located at the south-east corner of the site giving the effect of a tower at the junction of streets, and forming the other side of the courtyard. A pergola connects the old hall front door with the new church entrance. The final bay of the pergola is glazed in, acting as porch, and off this is a small chapel which frames the courtyard on the street side.

The bulk of the church, comprising a great polygonal tower, made of unadorned brickwork banded at regular intervals with stripes of concrete, is quite extraordinary in context. It is capped by a low double-pitched roof simply glazed at both gable ends; clustering around its base is a series of similar forms, with the same roofs leaning against each side of the polygon, each one increasing in height by a band of brickwork. The affinity between a 1960s church and the Victorian use of 'streaky bacon' brickwork a hundred years earlier was less surprising than it seems, since many architects of the New Brutalist generation admired the work of William Butterfield, one of the masters of coloured brick, for its rigour and avoidance of prettiness.

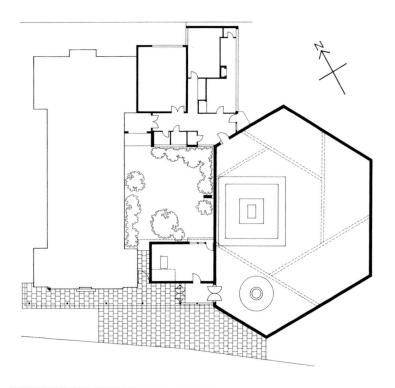

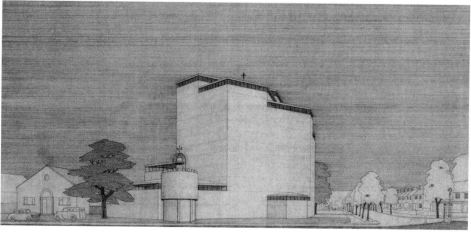

top: St Matthew's Church, Perry Beeches, Birmingham, plan
above: St Matthew's Church, perspective of first design based on a 'fractal' plan generation scheme
opposite top: St Matthew's Church, exterior
opposite centre: St Matthew's Church, font and furniture designed by Maguire & Murray
opposite lower: St Matthew's Church, interior up-view showing roof and lights

The pent roofs clustering around the base and spiralling upwards are raised up from their supporting walls beneath on thin strips of clerestory windows. This prepares us for the lighting effects in the spatially complex church interior. On entering through the porch, the font is directly ahead beneath the lowest of these monopitch roofs. To the left is the altar, aligned with the rear wall. These neat orthogonal relationships are countered by the overwhelming hexagonal geometry of the roof form, comprising a central regular hexagon and flanking semi-hexagons. It is a completely column-free space with the chord of each semi-hexagon a concrete beam matching the height of the brick bands. 'Central hexagon' is a misnomer: it is actually off-centre and abuts the long wall behind the altar, and it is this play of geometries, seemingly irreconcilable, that engenders a feeling of centrality to a space that also has to function as one side of a courtyard. The three-dimensional 'spiralling' of the roofs also means that you enter at the lowest point, lending an intimacy to the baptistery. The spiralling form ensures that the perimeter of the church is constantly bent back on itself, so that the font never feels far away, and is visible from everywhere. The quality of light lends the church a lively atmosphere, sufficiently luminous without being excessively numinous: Perry Beeches has no insincere religiosity to it. The gables of the topmost roof are glazed, giving enough illumination, and yet the horizontal slits of light beneath each pent roof mean that overemphatic contrasts are avoided, and the space remains well-lit throughout. Although its layout is based firmly on new liturgical principles, with the congregation gathering round the altar 'naturally', Perry Beeches is also a self-conscious work of art. In this Maguire and Murray were influenced by the writings of Geradus van der Leeuw, the Dutch professor of the history of religion, who sought to reunite art and religion, stressing the symbolic in art as did the American philosopher Suzanne Langer some twenty years later.[2]

Ethnic domains

Langer took her cue from her mentor, the German-Jewish philosopher Ernst Cassirer, on whose *Philosophy of Symbolic Forms* she built.[3] Her major book, *Philosophy in a New Key* (1942), led to a critique of art based on the theory of symbolism.[4] *Feeling and Form* was the result; published in 1953, it struck an immediate chord with practitioners of art and architecture.[5] It was anti-positivist in tone, phenomenological in its quest for meaning beyond the utilitarian and pragmatic, but couched in everyday, understandable language. Her principal contribution to architecture was to argue that its basic abstraction was what she termed an 'ethnic domain':

> *A place ... is a created thing, an ethnic domain made visible, tangible, sensible. ... The architectural illusion [of an ethnic domain] may be established by a mere array of upright stones defining the magic circle that severs holiness from the profane, even by a single stone that marks a center, i.e. a monument. The outside world, even though not physically shut out, is dominated by the sanctum and becomes its visible context; the horizon its frame.[6]*

These were ways of conceptualising the power of environment that exerted a great influence on Maguire and Murray. In a lecture given by them jointly in 1961 entitled 'Architecture and Christian Meanings' they contemplated that famous phrase from the Lord's Prayer 'Give us this day our daily bread', and wondered why a loaf of super-market sliced bread wouldn't do: 'It is simply because it has a symbolic content which is not expressive of … deep-rooted meanings. It is expressive of other values. It feels wrong. This is independent of whether or not the bread itself is good. It has to do with its look.'[7] Substance was later given to this phenomenological approach to architecture by the publication of a much-talked-about text of 1962, 'Towards making Places', by the American architect Charles Moore and collaborators, one of whom, Pat Quinn, was a close friend of Maguire's.[8] This article marked a certain turn in architecture towards the anthropological, coinciding with the *Team Ten Primer*, also published in 1962. Maguire would later restate his debt to Langer during his headship of the Oxford School of Architecture. He proposed that

> there is an 'art' aspect of architecture to achieve which the architect
> engages in certain kinds of activity, however little he knows it or wishes
> to acknowledge it. Every architect must surely admit that occasionally he
> fiddles with the position or proportion of a window, for example, in order
> to achieve some object about which he may or may not feel he is clear, but
> which he knows is dependent on his sensibility.[9]

At Perry Beeches, the door to the right of the altar as seen from the congregation is minor compared to the main entrance porch door, and is symptomatic of Maguire and Murray's wish to correct the 'leakage' of space experienced at St Paul's, Bow Common, where the peripheral wall was interrupted on too many occasions. This door leads to the rear entrance to the church, which also serves the vestry, parish office, meeting room and alternative way to the parish hall. A glazed wall in this entrance hall reveals the 'secret' courtyard garden for the first time, a space where there is a return to orthogonal, right-angle geometries. From the perspective of today, one might say the church was a 'fractal' scheme *avant la lettre*, and yet here, in contrast to much of what passes for parametric design today there is restraint and control exhibited on the part of the architects: they know when to desist from geometry for geometry's sake, so that the spiralling form evinces enclosure, focus and (spiritual) growth, whereas the more mundane parts of the building adjust and conform to the right angle, which, to use a phrase of Le Corbusier's, never becomes 'tyrannical'.

Reordering the church

Both Maguire and Murray continued their activities for the New Churches Research Group, and from 1962 to 1964 they assumed the joint role of editing *Churchbuilding*, the group's influential magazine. Their ideas regarding the layout of churches were tested in numerous reordering schemes; these were never about redecoration, but always sought to get to the heart of what it meant to worship today, whilst being sympathetic to the

top: Chapel of the Hostel of the Resurrection, Leeds, re-ordered
above: Chapel of the Hostel of the Resurrection, before re-ordering

architecture of the original. Such was their growing reputation that parishes would approach them when they felt that their style of worship – their liturgical practice – was impaired by limitations imposed by the architecture of their churches. These were generally nineteenth- and early twentieth-century layouts which grew out of the Victorian High Church Ecclesiological movement, rendering the laity submissive to a 'high priesthood'. This tended to make churches theatres of private devotion, inimical to the more inclusive, participatory liturgy of the second half of the twentieth century. In such churches the altar was positioned too far away from the congregants who were seated in immovable pews with views of other people's backs. The problem was how to adapt medieval or nineteenth-century churches for the kind of worship required today.

The architectural problem was one of context. 'Doing things in old churches', according to Maguire, 'was a "context" problem compressed, and required a developed philosophy. Other architects were either "keeping in keeping" (in varying degrees of plagiarism) or "uncompromisingly modern" (which meant imposing your artistic pretensions). Keith and I were completely agreed on the "light touch" – and devoid as much as consciously possible of "Style" – but our rearrangements were far more radical than [those of] the other guys.'[10] A good example of their approach was their reordering of the chapel of the Hostel of the Resurrection at Leeds in the mid-1960s, an object lesson in a 'less is more' approach, almost Miesian in its simplicity. A more recent example at St Mary's, Thame (1988–93) shows how removing the pews (a post-medieval innovation) and replacing them with concentric arcs of low chairs, focused on a new altar table in a more forward position, satisfied the requirements for a more

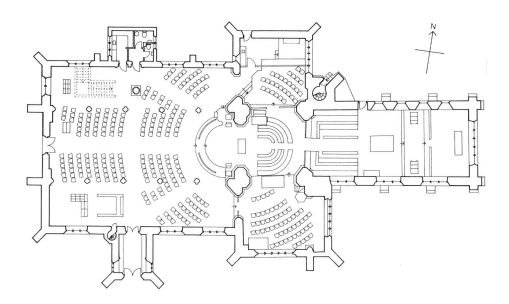

above: **St Mary's church, Thame, Oxfordshire, plan as re-ordered**

participatory, communal worship while being sympathetic to the original spatial tectonics of the medieval architecture.

Sometimes their intervention needed to involve adding elements. At St Thomas's, Heptonstall (1962–4) the large interior is humanised for worship by bringing the altar forward and separating a smaller, more intimate sanctuary by screening it off from other areas of the church used for social events. This organ screen is a powerful feature, of a scale and presence which copes well with its location, and is an example of an 'inhabited wall', containing organ loft above and two enclosures used as vestries beneath. The organ was designed by Maguire who had developed an interest in the design and construction of musical instruments since his student days. All the organs in the churches designed by Maguire & Murray were designed by Maguire, with the exception of the one at Bow Common, where the case alone was by him.

During this period of a burgeoning workload Maguire and Murray moved their office from Bloomsbury to Kew, a stone's throw from where the partners lived in the Fabyc community. They rented the lower parts of a Georgian house on Kew Green, and stayed there for ten years, until 1974.

above: **St Mary's church, Thame, diagonal view across interior**

West Malling

For Maguire and Murray, the all-enclosing wall was the initial architectonic fact to be established for a church. Continuous and with as few breaches as possible, it directed contemplation within oneself, and above, to the source of daylight. It delineated outside from inside, making the inside a place 'set apart' as Maguire was to put it in an article on Bow Common.[11] What would they make of a site that was already a walled enclave, a refuge from the hurly-burly of the world? Such was St Mary's Abbey at West Malling, Kent. This Anglican community of Benedictine nuns inhabited a walled garden behind the High Street, among the ruins of the great Norman church whose massive west tower survived the Reformation. They required a new cloister, a new range of cells; Maguire and Murray provided these, together with a new church.

The exterior form of the church presents itself as a closed volume, one which recalls the simple geometries of Romanesque work. A rectangular box of creamy-grey ballast blocks appears to support a smaller raised box with semicircular ends; a pitched roof above the ambulatory takes up the difference in size and shape. The church functions to all intents and purposes as a private chapel for the Anglican Benedictine order of nuns,

top left: Heptonstall church, West Yorkshire, organ screen
top right: St Mary's Abbey church, West Malling, seen behind the Romanesque tower

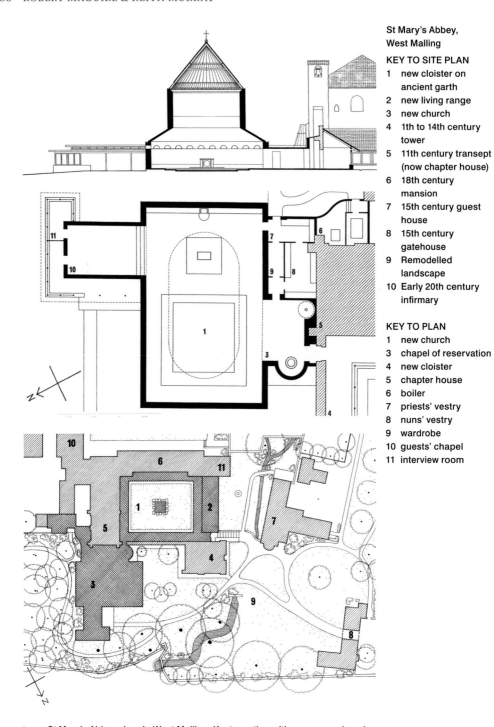

St Mary's Abbey,
West Malling

KEY TO SITE PLAN
1 new cloister on
   ancient garth
2 new living range
3 new church
4 1th to 14th century
   tower
5 11th century transept
   (now chapter house)
6 18th century
   mansion
7 15th century guest
   house
8 15th century
   gatehouse
9 Remodelled
   landscape
10 Early 20th century
   infirmary

KEY TO PLAN
1 new church
3 chapel of reservation
4 new cloister
5 chapter house
6 boiler
7 priests' vestry
8 nuns' vestry
9 wardrobe
10 guests' chapel
11 interview room

top: St Mary's Abbey church, West Malling, Kent, section with accompanying plan
above: St Mary's Abbey, site plan with new buildings in darker tone

and occupies a position roughly at the crossing of the old church. Despite its lowering mass it lacks any significant entrance portal, and does not incorporate the surviving west front into its circulation scheme. Instead Maguire and Murray devised a pair of low-ceilinged chapel-like spaces at opposite diagonals of the rectangular body of the church, one of which functions as ante-space for the nuns, off which is a niche accommodating the Sacrament House, with skylight above. This links cloister to church, while the other works as the visitors' prayer space. The church is organised so that the two geometrical foci relating to the great sweep of roof above define the zones of the choir (at the cloister end) and the altar (at the guests' end).

From the visitor's perspective, the effect is sublime. One takes one's seat, sees the priest at the altar, but can only hear the choir beyond. Only at the time of the Eucharist service do nuns and guests see each other, when all move into the space in front of the altar, forming a circle around the priest. In fact, the diagonal plan relationship (of rotational symmetry) of either end of the rectangular volume of the church works seamlessly to effect the level of privacy and discretion demanded by the nuns. This plan arrangement recurs frequently in the practice's work.

above: **St Mary's Abbey, aerial view**

Here is a Maguire and Murray church where, in comparison with its urban parochial counterparts, the lack of a legible 'entrance' presents no problem. The nuns are the principal worshippers and they see the church as an organic part of the complex of buildings and gardens in which they live, work and pray. The sequence of spaces through which guests enter from the gate is discreet, yet obvious. A clearly discernible path mediates between the perimeter wall on the left and the loosely defined axis formed by the west tower, the south transept and the new church. Critics loved the uncompromising aesthetic of the church. John Newman, in 'The Buildings of England' volume for West Kent wrote that 'The nuns wished for something simple and austere,

above: **St Mary's Abbey church, interior. The guests' chapel is just visible to the left of the altar**

top: St Mary's Abbey, western range of living accommodation
above: St Mary's Abbey, cloister

and that is what they have been given ...', although this is qualified by his perception that 'The lowering, shuttered-concrete ambulatory ceiling hovers overhead like a thundercloud ...'[12] Matters were hardly improved when columns were inserted in the early 1970s at the junction of the sloping ambulatory ceiling and the clerestory below the lantern in a successful attempt to counter secondary forces not foreseen by the consultant engineer.

If the church has structural gymnastics framing an austere aesthetic, the range of residential accommodation and the cloister offer sweetness and light. The cloister is medieval in its character, an unheated space with glazing to the garden within. The pattern of elongated hexagonal lozenges in lead cames in the windows was criticised as 'fussy tea-shoppe glazing' by Nicholas Taylor, but the windows themselves are off-centred pivots, such that when fully open, at right-angles to the cloister wall, they correspond exactly to the edge of roof eaves above, and form screened seats for the nuns.[13] A further sophistication is the introduction of a gap between the main beam and the timber plate bearing the rafters. A series of wooden 'cotton-reels' serves to lighten the junction visually, mitigating the gloomy atmosphere within the cloister. The various items of quirky and unprecedented detailing lighten the cloister and make an uncannily good fit with the medieval ambience of the abbey without resorting to pastiche.

Architecture and poverty

During Maguire and Murray's joint editorship of the journal *Churchbuilding* between 1962 and 1964 it adopted a much more questioning stance than previously, and was modelled on the stylish and influential French publication *L'Art Sacré*. In 1962, *Churchbuilding* reprinted 'Transparent Poverty', an essay by the young Swiss architect Rainer Senn, originally published in *L'Art Sacré* in 1958 and commented on by the *Architects' Journal* in 1960.[14] Senn's other contribution to *Churchbuilding* was titled 'He planted his tent amongst us: the problem of economical churches'. This related to Senn's most famous project, a church outside Nice for a community of rag-pickers, designed as a simple wooden tent raised up on a square plan of timber walls at a cost of £50. Senn maintained that 'the limitation of financial means generally has a positive effect on the appearance of a building', a maxim he applied to all buildings; specifically in the case of churches, he 'tried to arrange the seats about a 'centre' and to emphasise this centre by spatial means and by the use of specially directed light'. His aim was that 'each individual should be aware on the one hand of his togetherness with others and on the other hand of his relationship to a common centre.'[15] Senn's work was also illustrated by Peter Hammond in his book *Towards a Church Architecture* in pages immediately following illustrations of the Bow Common and Perry Beeches churches. While these statements of Senn's clearly apply to the churches at Bow Common and Perry Beeches, the spare aesthetic and tent-like form of St André are most visible at the next Maguire and Murray church, All Saints, Crewe (1962–7).

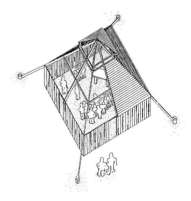

above: Chapel at Saint-André, near Nice, France, Rainer Senn, 1955

All Saints, Crewe

Crewe is a railway town of trim redbrick terraced and semi-detached houses, and All Saints is located to the west of the town centre on a slightly wedge-shaped rectangular site, running east–west from the residential Stewart Street. The site is squared off by a continuous range of building comprising, from east (Stewart Street) to west, the church, entrance hall, parish hall and finally the vicarage. These form a wall of Staffordshire blue brickwork nestling beneath a common asbestos-cement slate roof which is only interrupted by the cut that signals the entrance. This great sweep of roof makes three right-angled turns over the church to form a low-pitched pyramidal roof, the apex of which is raised upon a simple clerestory of square windows. While hall and house have their walls meeting the roof to form a normal eaves detail, the perimeter wall of the church is set back by a metre from the roof edge which oversails it, forming deep, cantilevered eaves. The four corners of the church are boldly rounded, with one mysterious convex bulge in the north-east wall near the entrance. If the external form is reminiscent of Senn's pyramid form, the materials are absolutely of the north-west, as if this were a stylistically neutral contemporary rendering of a tough, industrial vernacular, conjuring up the 'functional tradition' beloved of Maguire's former boss at the Architectural Press, J. M. Richards.

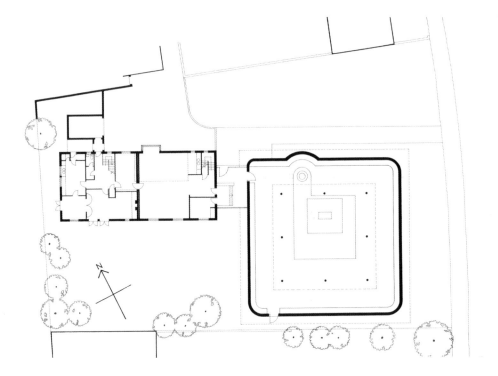

above: All Saints church, Crewe, plan/ site plan
opposite: All Saints church, interior showing font

However, our expectations within a goods shed or metal workshop are immediately dispelled on entering the church. The scale is far more intimate than the exterior suggests and its materials are warmer. All this is revealed in extremely well-handled natural light.

The internal envelope diverges from the geometry of the external pyramid, with a flat ceiling above the clerestory, and a kind of pent – and bent – roof spanning between the perimeter wall and the ring beam beneath the high-level clerestory. The flat, low soffit to this roof sits on timber beams at 6 m centres spanning between the outer wall and white-painted circular-section hollow steel columns. Although it is not immediately obvious, the roof actually stands above this wall, spaced off it by a narrow but continuous strip of window, similar to that seen in the cloister at West Malling. Four of these columns stake out the centre of the church, beneath the raised pyramid roof, with one additional column on each of the four sides. On entering the church the font is directly ahead. It is this which causes the ripple in the fabric of the church, forcing the bulge in the perimeter wall. The font is close to the grouping of altar and pulpit, yet located outside the central square as defined by the columns and clerestory. Short, low pews seating 250 surround the altar on three sides, with a continuous bench against the wall accommodating a further 150 people.

At Crewe, Maguire and Murray reverted to a ciborium over the altar, a spare, thin tubular affair with a fabric awning – altogether less monumental than its precursor at Bow Common. Its design marks something of a transition for the practice. Having established their liturgical reform credentials, they were now striving to make their

top: **All Saints church, interior with ciborium over altar**

churches convivial, 'normal' buildings which related well in material and formal terms to their physical contexts while fostering social aspects of communities within, having satisfied their spiritual needs. For the *Architects' Journal* reviewer, All Saints was '...
a very different building from either Bow Common or Perry Beeches. These churches both have an element of tough "protest" about them, of the kind which led to comparisons with Butterfield. All Saints is a gentler, more domestic conception, and it shows a rare feeling for the quality of the nineteenth-century urban environment.'[16]

Community and liturgy

Who knows what commissions might have resulted had parish reorganisation in the diocese of Ely not taken place, with the subsequent abandonment of Maguire and Murray's scheme for a new church at Cherry Hinton, on the outskirts of Cambridge. Saint James's on Wulfstan Way merged the qualities of Bow Common and Perry Beeches. A four-square, orthogonal tower rose over the sanctuary, surrounded by an upward-spiralling succession of pent roofs with glazing in the gables. However, the

above: **All Saints church, exterior**

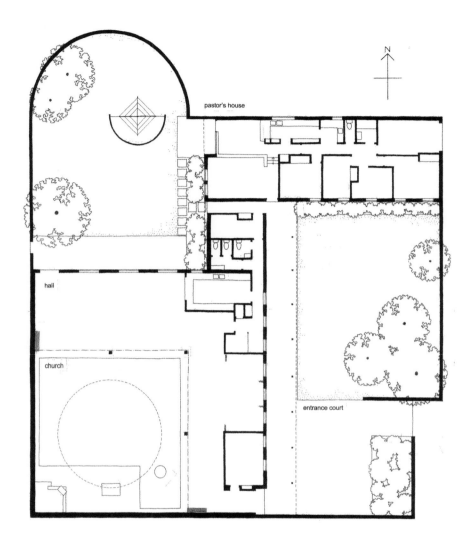

other church designed by the practice in 1963, the Church of the Redeemer at Tye Green in Harlow, was carried through to completion. Built for the (Canadian) Evangelical Lutheran Church, it had as unprepossessing a location as the preceding churches, but the client was different. This church was a departure for Maguire and Murray: a low spread of building across the square site with courtyards dispersed through the plan, with everything enclosed by a protecting wall. Serge Chermayeff and Christopher Alexander's book *Community and Privacy: towards an architecture of humanism* was published in the same year, a paean to the principles of 'patio' planning, where a

top: **Church of the Redeemer, Tye Green, Harlow, plan**

patchwork of indoor and outdoor spaces offers a careful hierarchy of private and semi-private spaces, spreading the benefits of open space more or less evenly through a building. It is a principle that argues against the idea of freestanding 'object' buildings, and for the continuity of built fabric epitomised by the traditional city. Religious complexes frequently demonstrate such homogeneity of building. Abbey complexes offer rich examples, including West Malling where church, cloister, cells and baptistery are all attached one to another.

The church at Tye Green is a good deal smaller than its predecessors. The congregation sits within a square defined by the south and west walls of the church, and by a colonnade on the other two sides. This sits within a greater square, where the church hall and ancillary spaces are located forming a kind of ambulatory. Entrance is from the east into a small courtyard defined by 'Miesian' walls at right-angles to each other, redolent of Maguire's student church project. Passing through a colonnade which

above: **Church of the Redeemer**

extends north to frame a planted courtyard, you enter the church proper. The pastor's house lies to the north of the courtyard garden, and completing the composition, at the north-west corner of the walled enclosure, is another garden. This can be reached directly from the church hall. The plan is one of the most satisfying of all Maguire and Murray's churches in its seemingly effortless control of space and movement. If you want to see 'pinwheel' planning at its best, look no further.

This may be compared to Maguire and Murray's other Lutheran church in London, in the basement of their International Lutheran Centre (1974–8). It has a formal entrance from Sandwich Street in the form of a simple semicircular doorway reminiscent of Louis Sullivan or the early Frank Lloyd Wright. Indeed, there are echoes of Wright's Unity Temple, Oak Park, Chicago, in the coffered flat ceiling of the church. Spatial and elemental motifs similar to those encountered at their earlier churches abound. A diagonal relationship is set up in the plan that encourages a spiralling, anticlockwise movement around the ambulatory. The sanctuary is defined by a rectangle of 3 x 4 bays of reinforced concrete columns; the organ, designed by Maguire, occupies one of these bays in the vicinity of the altar, a moveable table which can be moved back to the wall behind when the space is converted to work as a meeting room. The organ is balanced by a convex semicircular wall that harbours a meditation space ('chapel' would be too grand a term) behind.

above: Lutheran Centre, Bloomsbury, London, church

In many respects the influence of Maguire and Murray's church planning had become widespread by the end of the decade; certainly their ideas on 'the liturgical plan' had been digested by the clergy, if not by all congregants. A new concern for this period was for participation in its widest sense, and not simply in terms of the Eucharist. Churches might have the potential to be community centres, and not just for the faithful. At the end of the 1960s they designed two new churches on the suburban edges of London and Manchester respectively, where they sought to give appropriate emphasis to their community function as much as to their spiritual role.

St Philip's and St James's Church, Hodge Hill, Birmingham, 1968, designed by Martin Purdy was a response to the Birmingham theologian John Gordon Davies whose book *The Secular Use of Church Buildings* was published in 1968.[17] The book sought to demystify church architecture to such an extent that it rendered churches indistinguishable from schools, community centres or youth clubs.[18] The church at Hodge Hill is seen as perhaps '… the logical progression of the ideals of the Liturgical Movement, with its call for greater openness. But architecturally, as well as spiritually, the result has too often been divisive and a debasement of the sense of place that is as important to the religious and the agnostic alike.'[19] This drive towards flexibility, a buzz-word of the late 1960s and early 1970s, was a step too far for Maguire and Murray: they still insisted on a place 'set apart' for the Eucharist, arguing that, to be consistent, you may as well use the school hall and a trestle-table, and save a lot of money.

Re-pitching the tent[20]

On Yeading Lane in Northolt, an interwar West London suburb on the flight path into Heathrow, the parish of St Joseph the Worker was set up in the 1940s, operating out of a hall-cum-church. The population was solidly working class, finding employment in local light industry and in the nearby airport. Indeed, much of the post-war population came from inner West London, a reminder to Maguire of his own Paddington roots. The triangular site directly off the busy road (the 'Lane' is a misnomer) allowed for a layout that amalgamated the best features of Tye Green's courtyard planning with the presence of Crewe. A long wall forms the boundary along the street to the north of the site; behind this, stretching out to the southwest, are ranged the priest's house and church hall, separated by the vicarage garden. Beyond these is set the square plan of the church, but 'slipped' so that it is lodged within the community facilities, while at the same time setting up two distinct zones on the perimeter, the one on Yeading Lane for car parking, the other to the south for pedestrian entrance. The congregation had traditional views regarding what a church should comprise: it insisted on a freestanding belfry which was initially resisted by Maguire and Murray who eventually relented. It is good they did, as the tower (3.66 m diameter and 13.1 m high) marks the church on the Lane, and defines the south-west corner. Another 'traditional' feature is the separate baptistery; located between the entrance hall and the church, and four steps below the level of the church, it sets up an axis with the chapel. Both these spaces are contained within semicircular apsidal forms which are complemented by the convex half-drum of the cloakroom 'pod'. The curved enclosure to the baptistery is actually formed by a low-level slate sill which continues into the church, where it becomes a bench surrounding the whole church, increasing its seating capacity substantially.

As befits St Joseph *qua* Worker, and making no bones about the congregants' blue-collar status, the aesthetic recalls that of the factory. As Nigel Melhuish put it in his review in the *Architects' Journal*, 'everything about Northolt – its shapes, materials, its grouping on the site – makes unambiguous reference to the familiar world of wage packets and productivity deals.'[21] Suddenly we are back in Harold Wilson's Britain of the late 1960s. Low concrete block perimeter walls are surmounted by zinc-clad walls and roofs, while inside the effect of All Saints, Crewe is heightened and refined. The section is, as it were, compressed so that the spreading low-pitch ambulatory roof becomes a

above left: **Church of St Joseph the Worker, Northolt**
above right: **Church of St Joseph the Worker: interior**

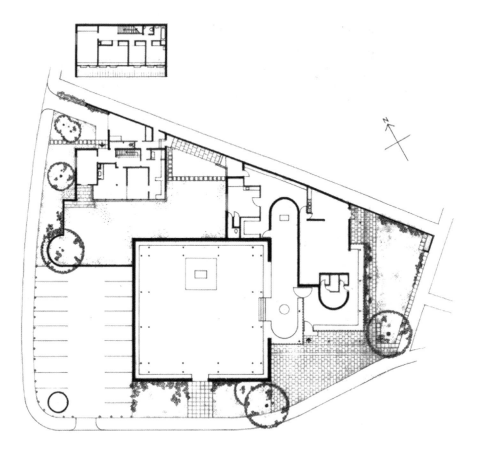

just-off-vertical wall, with pitched patent-glazing separating it from the low blockwork wall below and the flat timber roof above. This subtle building envelope, in addition to the excellent daylighting it affords, has a supporting structure which is elegant (white-painted circular steel tubes) while suggesting an ambulatory zone by virtue of its twin-legged form. It marks a transition for Maguire and Murray to using structural and constructional form explicitly in order to generate a building's aesthetic – High-Tech before that term had common currency.

While the planning of the church complex is formally brilliant, with its carefully controlled play of axes and cross-axes, right-angles and semicircles, its succession of very precise and functionally 'correct' spaces has been subverted by subsequent use and

above: **Church of St Joseph the Worker, ground and site plan (with first floor plan of vicarage)**

conversions. The baptistery is no more, its space (but not its form) having made way for an enlarged entrance hall-cum-coffee lounge. This kind of communal function was not part of the original liturgical reform brief, but it is instructive to note that Maguire and Murray's tough church can deal with the more evangelical tone of its current congregants, in the same way that the many medieval and Gothic Revival churches reordered by the practice have lives beyond the original vision of their clerics, builders and designers.

In an article written by Maguire and Murray for *Churchbuilding* in 1966 the architects talked about design for expandability.[22] The four-square church described in the article has top-hung pivoting wall sections below the ring of clerestory glazing; these can be raised to allow for an augmented congregation to be accommodated. The section is reminiscent of the canted walls of St Joseph's, and lends the church an aura of the transitory, an external tent envelope encompassing the community. So contemporary buildings for the Church should, in the eyes of such Christian socialists as Maguire and Murray, be made in the image of the 'poverty' of Christianity, where instead of the voluptuous sensuality of, say, St Peter's in Rome or Richard Meier's Roman church *Dio Padre Misericordioso*, 1996–2003, you have the simplicity of a Shaker barn in New England. This accorded well with the kind of client of limited means that Maguire and Murray tended to encounter.

above: **Church of St Joseph the Worker, Northolt, baptistery**

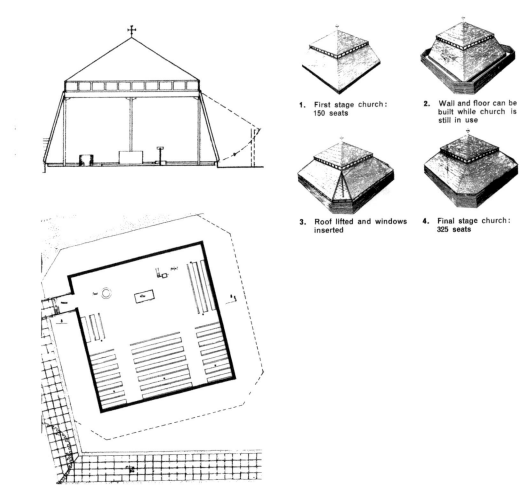

1. First stage church:
   150 seats

2. Wall and floor can be
   built while church is
   still in use

3. Roof lifted and windows
   inserted

4. Final stage church:
   325 seats

Hulme roofs

The final church in this series, not completed until 1972, was the Church of the
Ascension, Hulme, Manchester. Hulme was infamous for its wholesale reconstruction
in the 1960s where within a decade the four giant deck-access blocks of flats, designed
by Hugh Wilson and J. L. Womersley, had become a modern slum, rundown and
uninhabitable, and were demolished before the end of the century. The church offered
a refuge within this turbulent environment, literally so in 1986 when a Tamil refugee,
Viraj Mendis, found shelter from an extradition order, and remained within the church
for two years.

above: 'Expanding' church

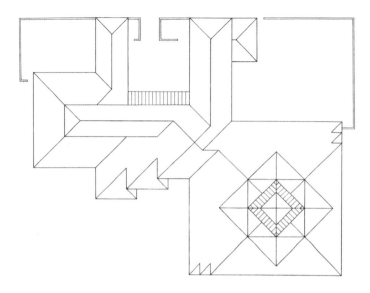

In order not to compete with the strident and brutal estate in which it was placed, the church is low and spreading – a pinwheel, orthogonal plan with entrance hall right in the centre. Indeed, its extravagantly geometrical roof was designed to be seen from the adjacent flats that loomed above it. Spinning off from this, triskelion fashion, are the three limbs of vicarage, church and meeting hall, with four courtyards or gardens filling in. The theme of rotational symmetry continues inside the church; the sanctuary in the southeast corner is faced by three blocks of bench seating, with a fourth block to the north. This L-shaped configuration is mirrored by a gallery sitting above two sides of the ambulatory, serving to make a more intimate space for the baptistery below the short leg, and a place for a semi-enclosed chapel in the other. This is the only instance of a gallery in a Maguire and Murray church; it makes for a more intimate church and gives space for a proper organ loft. The plan geometry sounds obsessive, but is not perceived as such, having the ease of a classic pinwheel plan.

Where the geometry does verge on the obsessive is the roof whose 45° beam structure is revealed as the insistent ceiling pattern. It is a modern version of the kitchen of the Romanesque abbey of Fontevrault in the Loire valley or of an Anatolian bathhouse; its repetition and piling-up of forms create a jewel-box of a building. Indeed, this analogy is heightened by the zinc cladding that sparkles and glistens. It marks the beginning of a small series of expressionist, geometrical roof forms designed by the practice: the Garden Room at Kew (1969–70) was contemporary with Hulme, while the Governing Body Room, Worcester College, Oxford (1988–90) followed some twenty years later.

above: 'Church of the Ascension, roof plan

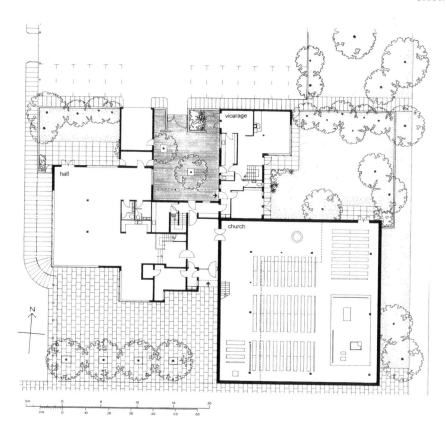

top: Church of the Ascension, Hulme, Manchester, ground floor and site plan
above: Church of the Ascension, exterior view from west

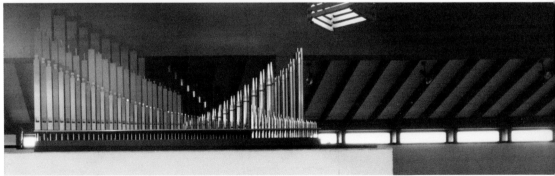

top: Church of the Ascension, interior
above: Church of the Ascension, organ designed by Robert Maguire

Some Roman Catholic churches

St Augustine's Roman Catholic church, Tunbridge Wells (1972–76) had a more
orthodox plan, with its altar positioned some 4 m away from the east wall, on the
short axis of the rectangular plan, and at the junction of the generous ambulatory
and 'sanctuary' – actually the central zone of the church – staked out by four white-
painted circular-section steel columns bearing a 'table' of great steel beams, a kind of
scaled-up ciborium. This bold structure then supports a much finer construction of
green-stained rafters and tie beams, at such close centres that they create a forest-like
density through which daylight filters from the two by now familiar sources: a low-level,
narrow clerestory where external wall meets eaves, and higher up, at either gable end,
where the gablets afford vertical glazing. Without and within, St Augustine's gives the
impression of being a great barn, a sophisticated semi-rural one in its landscape setting
on the fringes of Decimus Burton's neo-classical Calverley Park Estate. This unerring
sensitivity to physical context continues the Maguire and Murray approach of dressing
their 'big barns' appropriately: at Crewe, by reference to the heritage of the Industrial
Revolution, at Northolt to contemporary imagery of the factory.

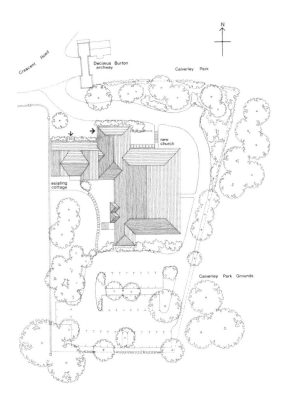

above: St Augustine's church, Tunbridge Wells, Kent, site plan

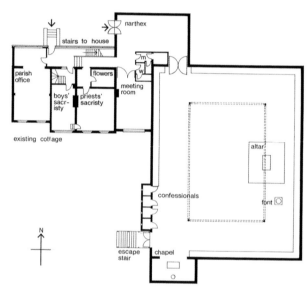

top: St Augustine's church, exterior
middle: St Augustine's church, upper ground floor plan
above: St Augustine's church, interior

top: St Bede's church, Basingstoke, external view
above: St Bede's church, internal view

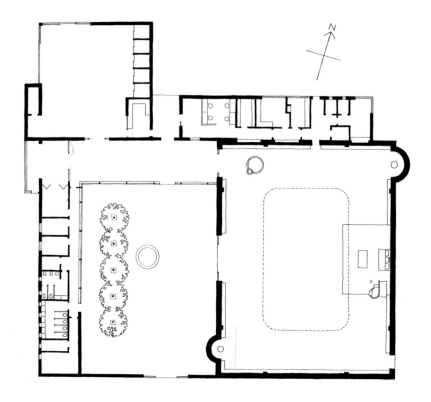

The final church scheme by Robert Maguire, designed under the aegis of Maguire & Co, and completed by JBKS Architects after Maguire's retirement, was St Bede's Roman Catholic Church, Basingstoke (2002–7). In its suburban site it takes the form of a great elongated pyramid with low eaves sitting on block walls. While it has a similar volume to that of St Augustine's Tunbridge Wells, it has a simplicity and grandeur which recalls the Abbey church at West Malling.

The church, as building type and as institution, was what made Maguire and Murray, and was the locus of their initial architectural investigations. If their focus was on the Eucharist, on the twin memory of sacrifice and communion, then teaching came next. What was the appropriate setting for teaching (and not just Christian teaching), and how could architectural design foster and represent it convincingly? This forms the next area of investigation, and rounds off the trio of building types that Maguire and Murray sought to understand and reinterpret.

above: **St Bede's church, Basingstoke, Hampshire, plan**

Notes

1   Peter Hammond, 'A Liturgical Brief', *Architectural Review*, April 1958, p.242.

2   Geradus van der Leeuw, *Sacred and Profane Beauty: the holy in art*, Oxford: Oxford University Press, 1963, trans. David E. Green. First published in Dutch in 1932.

3   Ernst Cassirer, *The Philosophy of Symbolic Forms. Volume 4, The Metaphysics of Symbolic Forms*, John Michael Krois and Donald Philip Verene, (eds), New Haven and London: Yale University Press, 1996, trans. John Michael Krois.

4   Suzanne Langer, *Philosophy in a New Key*, Cambridge, MA: Harvard University Press, 1942.

5   Suzanne Langer, *Feeling and Form*, New York: Scribner's, 1953.

6   ibid., p.95.

7   Robert Maguire and Keith Murray, 'Architecture and Christian Meanings', *Studia Liturgica*, June 1962.

8   Donlyn Lyndon, Charles W. Moore, Patrick J. Quinn & Sim van Der Ryn, 'Toward Making Places', *Landscape* 12, no. 1 (Autumn 1962), and 'Team Ten Primer' (1953–62) in *Architectural Design*, December 1962.

9   Robert Maguire, 'A Conflict between Art and Life?', Byron Mikellides, (ed.), *Architecture for People*, London: Studio Vista, 1980, pp.126 and 129.

10   From unpublished notes on reordering written by Robert Maguire.

11   Robert Maguire, 'Anglican Church in Stepney', *Churchbuilding*, October 1962, No. 7, p.15.

12   John Newman, *The Buildings of England: West Kent and the Weald*, Harmondsworth: Penguin, 1969; p.577.

13   Nicholas Taylor, 'Historic patterns', *Architectural Review*, November 1966, p.339.

14   'The churches of Rainer Senn', *Architects' Journal*, 28 April 1960, pp.646–51.

15   Rainer Senn, 'The Spirit of Poverty', *Churchbuilding* 9 (1963), p.63, trans. Keith Harrison. The two articles in *L'Art Sacré* were 'La Transparence de la Pauvreté', January/February 1958, and 'Il a planté sa tente parmi nous: Le problème des églises économiques', July/August 1958.

16   Building Appraisal, *Architects' Journal*, 4 September 1968, p.455.

17   John Gordon Davies, *The Secular Use of Church Buildings*, London: SCM Press, 1968.

18   See Elain Harwood, 'Liturgy and Architecture: The Development of the Centralised Eucharistic Space', *The Twentieth Century Church, Twentieth Century Architecture 3, The Journal of the Twentieth Century Society* (1998), pp.49–74.

19   ibid., p.74.

20   Richard Giles, *Repitching the Tent: re-ordering the church building for worship and mission in the new millennium*, Norwich: Canterbury Press, 1996.

21   Nigel Melhuish, *Architects' Journal*, 8 July 1970, p.79.

22   Robert Maguire and Keith Murray, 'Expandable Churches', *Churchbuilding*, January 1966, p.5.

4 School

*In the beginning man created the hall. It was not altogether without form,
and it was certainly not void. On the contrary, all human life was gathered
within it, eating and drinking and carousing and sleeping and engaging in
almost all the activities for which one needed a roof.*[1]
Andor Gomme and Alison Maguire, *Design and Plan in the Country House*, 2008

For the first ten years of their partnership, until the late 1960s, Maguire and Murray
concentrated on designing churches, together with some student housing. Their work
for Trinity College, Oxford represented a specialised area of educational building, but
they were eager to work on the design of schools, in view of their general approach and
because they were much involved with the schooling of their own young children.

Gresham Kirkby, the vicar of St Paul's, Bow Common, who enjoyed such a fruitful
relationship with both Robert Maguire and Keith Murray, became effectively the chairman
of governors of a Church of England primary school, for pupils aged 4–11, which required a
new building. It consisted of three infants' groups (of 40 pupils each), four juniors' (again of
40), plus a 40-place nursery section, making a total of 320. Father Kirkby was keen to renew
and continue the professional relationship with the architects, believing that they would
apply to education the kind of fresh thinking that they had brought to bear on liturgical
matters. The new school had two clients, the Diocese of London and the Inner London
Education Authority (ILEA), the schools' arm of the Greater London Council (GLC). The
ILEA had a well-deserved reputation for radicalism in all areas of education, and in 1969
when Maguire and Murray were commissioned to design St Paul's School, the radical
Pimlico School was nearing completion. Designed by the GLC under the leadership of the
architect John Bancroft, Pimlico offered a state-of-the-art comprehensive school whose
exterior expanses of concrete walling, canted patent glazing and boxy protruberances were
symbols of their time. The school was equally significant for its internal planning in the
form of an indoor street, a device adopted in the 1980s by some of the famous Hampshire
schools developed under the County Architect, (Sir) Colin Stansfield Smith.

Plowden and after

In 1967, Bridget (Lady) Plowden, chair of the Central Advisory Council on Education,
was asked by the government to report on primary school education and to make
recommendations to improve it. 'Children and their Primary Schools' was the outcome.

opposite: **St Paul's School, lunchtime**

The report did for primary education what the Robbins report had done for the
tertiary sector three years earlier. The two reports were, though, different in import:
without Robbins there would not have been the great expansion of higher education
in the UK; Plowden was more retrospective, in that advances had been taking place
in primary education since the beginning of the century. It gave official endorsement
to child-centred theory and practice in pedagogy. It was symptomatic of the overall
educational drive within the United Kingdom in the 1960s where, notwithstanding
the excellence that existed in the private sector, great swathes of deprived parts of the
country languished in underfunded and unenlightened conditions. The Plowden Report
urged systematic nursery education, recognising that many of the negative learning
and behavioural patterns of children were already in place by the time they reached
infants' school, aged five. It argued for increased resources to be directed to schools in
poor areas, but most importantly it rethought the curriculum, coming out against rote
learning in favour of stimulating children's innate curiosity about the world. It was the
design implications of this that would affect architects.

The Report makes for fascinating reading. For architects, Chapter 28: 'Primary
School Buildings and Equipment' tells the story of the shift from learning by rote to
learning by doing. The section illustrates a few schools as exemplars, in addition to the
plan layouts and relationship diagrams drawn up in the Building Bulletins published
by the Department of Education. The two actual schools illustrated are Finmere in
Oxfordshire (1958–59) and Eveline Lowe in Bermondsey, London (1965–66). Though
a modest, rural school, Finmere had salient elements that would recur at St Paul's: a
compact, squarish, deep plan, with teaching areas pushed out to the periphery around
a central hall-cum-gym space.[2] This kind of plan effectively banished the corridor from
the school. The Eveline Lowe School is much larger, and has a linear layout.[3] Completed
just before Maguire & Murray were commissioned at Bow Common, it had many of the
characteristics and attributes championed by Plowden which would find their way into
the design of St Paul's:

> (a) *The need to sub-divide the available space to allow a number of small
> groups of individuals to pursue widely varying activities.*
> (b) *The need to make a distinction in character (i.e. in finishes, scale, colour,
> lighting, furniture) between a small, quiet carpeted area; a general working
> area; and an area equipped for messier kinds of work.*
> (c) *The importance of direct access to a sheltered verandah and to the
> ground outside.*
> (d) *The need to take into account the use of sizes of furniture from an early
> stage in design process.*
> *There is no hard and fast division between these group spaces and the rest
> of the school, for the whole environment (both inside and out) was conceived
> as potential 'teaching space', as opposed to a series of closed classrooms and
> 'non-teaching' areas.*[4]

The last sentence is perhaps the most crucial, and the one that Maguire and Murray would latch onto wholeheartedly with the design of St Paul's. In many respects it out-Plowdens the findings of the report, setting a wholly new paradigm for school building in terms of both educational ethos and architectural expression.

The finest modern barn in England

State school provision was undertaken according to stringent cost guidelines, with a budget determined by the number of pupils, at a standard level. If they were to adopt the Plowden principles, Maguire and Murray's initial task lay in maximising space per pupil within the cost limit. There were two principal ways of achieving this: by reducing circulation areas, and by minimising the cost of the building envelope. Very early on in the design process the architects hit upon a simple, wide-span agricultural shed as the basic building form. In 1967 they had begun work on designing a riding school north of Oxford. Although this came to nothing, it acquainted Maguire and Murray with standard portal frame structures and their low cost, 'a poor man's Bucky dome', to quote Maguire.[5] Bow Common comprised six low-pitched steel portal structures, propped by columns at approximately quarter-span. The low spreading roof sheltered a largely open-plan arrangement beneath, but with a clear pattern of use. The lowest parts of the roof housed the teaching areas: in Plowden-speak, 'home bays' with their 'resource areas'; on the west side are the juniors and on the east the infants, partially enclosed by high and low screen walls respectively. These areas gave out directly onto the wide covered play areas – at some 4 m, they were far more than token verandas, and offered real usable space, further expanding the children's realm during all but the coldest days of the year.

In its original condition, larger communal spaces were located along the north–south axis, beneath the roof-ridge: the assembly hall (doubling as gymnasium) to the south, and the dining area in the centre. At the northern end of the building was the kitchen, above which was the staff mezzanine (with library). Rooflights flush with the asbestos-cement roof provided good general illumination, boosted by fluorescent battens. The thermal insulation was reversed according to its normal manner of instal-lation, with its integral leaf of aluminium foil placed facing downwards, increasing the reflectivity of the ceiling. It was held in place by the simple expedient of white-painted garden trellis. The 'barn' was heated by a centrally located, high-level ducted warm air heating and ventilation system, operating in conjunction with a more conventional perimeter radiator system. One could say that 'the silver finish glittering through the garden trellis transforms what would otherwise be an agricultural aesthetic into something akin to a fairground or magical grotto' and gives a rather pop art feeling to the space, as if we were in a painting by Peter Blake.[6] In the next decade an open-plan school might have been rendered High Tech, with architects pursuing their art for art's sake; not so at Bow Common. Indeed, there is a curious double-take – some might say equivocation – going on here, because against the backdrop of the rather unfinished, *brut,* structure and fabric came an overlay of strong, vibrant colour, frequently in stripes, as if Bridget Riley were let loose on the farm.

Bow Common School was all rather unprecedented when it was opened in 1972. It was said that Lady Plowden herself had to intervene in order to get it through some of the administrative hoops.[7] The nature of its innovation was misunderstood, and according to Maguire 'it's not open plan, it's open section'.[8] This was not the first open-plan primary school, but it was the first to take the concept to its logical

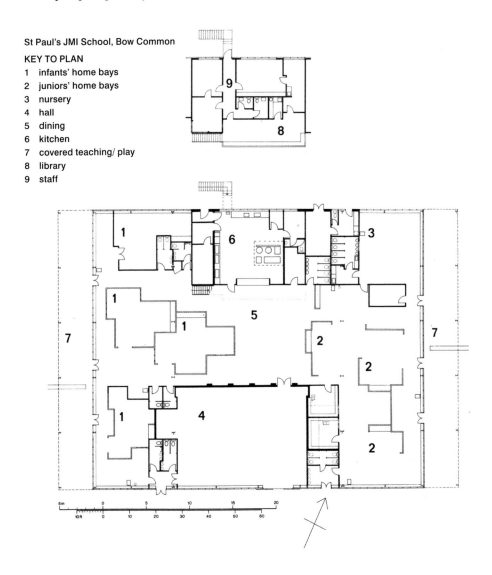

St Paul's JMI School, Bow Common

KEY TO PLAN
1   infants' home bays
2   juniors' home bays
3   nursery
4   hall
5   dining
6   kitchen
7   covered teaching/ play
8   library
9   staff

above: St Paul's School, Bow Common, London, plans

top: St Paul's School, exterior
above: Bow Common School interior

conclusion, instead of simply removing some walls from a conventionally planned, cellular scheme. On an extremely tight budget, it provided almost 20 per cent more floor-space per pupil than a conventional school.

Students' Union, Surrey

The critical success of Stag Hill Court in 1970, including the approval of its users, led to the University inviting Maguire and Murray to design its Students' Union building. The site was at the eastern end of the rectilinear grid of academic buildings, before the land sloped down to Stag Hill Court. The master plan by Building Design Partnership (BDP) typified the architecture of the new university in the late 1960s. It was coolly rational, a pattern of horizontal glazed expanses, interrupted at intervals by concrete circulation towers. Maguire and Murray's Students' Union offered a different expression, mediating between the scale and massing of the academic buildings to the north-west, and the more intimate character of their own housing to the south.

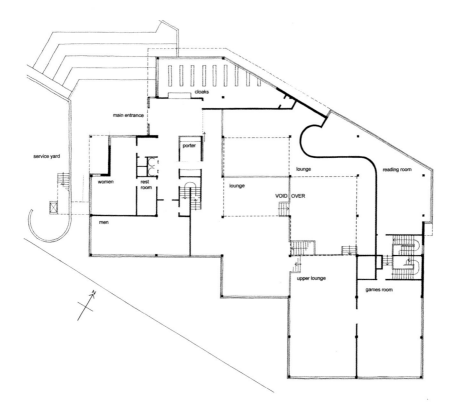

above: Students' Union building, Surrey University, Guildford, plan at entrance level

The site forms a hinge whose north flank aligns with a major pedestrian path running east–west, while the rest of the building turns through some 40°. In this way its southern sawtooth edge matches the geometry of the housing opposite, its echelon form setting up a relationship with the staggered layout of Stag Hill Court. A broad, paved plaza rises gradually to form a stepped, hard landscape, leading up to a right-angled semi-courtyard, where the 'front door' to the Union is located. This external space is a significant informal amphitheatre in the campus, more laid back than BDP's more imposing space in front of the Senate to the west, where it is framed by tree foliage in the foreground with a distant view of Maufe's cathedral tower at the end of the picturesque vista. The Union building has the geometry of Stag Hill Court, and a scale which is far more intimate than that of the corporate BDP buildings to the north and west. This intimacy is achieved by very skilful site planning, with the bulk of the main hall in the Union located downhill, below the entrance level.

The materials resemble those of Stag Hill – buff-coloured concrete blocks, square-faced for a finer facade texture – while the overall form gives the impression of triangular gables capped off by horizontals as with the housing. This is sleight of hand, though, because the Union is a relatively deep-plan building of flat roofs which stagger down and across the plan,

above: **Students' Union building, external view, with Stag Hill Court housing to the right**

top: Students' Union building, music gig
above: Students' Union building, daylit interior

in step with the south echelon edge of the form itself. Timber-framed strip windows lend a horizontal emphasis and a coherence to the otherwise fragmented building; the topmost strip of fenestration, however, comprises aluminium windows, akin to patent glazing, surmounted by zinc siding and sloping glazing. The effect is to lighten the appearance of the top of the building, and to decrease its bulk. Inside, the building reveals itself to be a three-dimensional kasbah, a lively and densely packed advice centre, music venue and complex of drinking bars of differing natures, descending via half-levels around a large central volume. This is the events venue, the place for live music and discos. It is framed by a dark-painted steel structure, with a plethora of galleries with white-slatted balustrades. It is a place of great atmosphere at night, a kind of Elizabethan or Jacobean galleried theatre pit, but equally a generous and naturally lit forum by day. The steel frame gives way to a timber structure for the roof, a complicated and intricate essay in the art of the carpenter. Gang-nailed trussed rafters abound, with the lower tie joists continuing, with long,

above: Students' Union building, internal roof structure

bulkhead light-fittings attached to each joist end. Rafters are propped off the supporting steel joists by 'cotton-reels', lengths of pitch-fibre drainpipe, a similar detail to that encountered at the cloister glazing at West Malling Abbey. The spatial effect is one of complexity and homogeneity – an intricacy speaking of student community and politics, a world away from the more corporate, 'polite' world of the University administration next door.

The open section

This uncanny ability to summon up, reflect and express the life of the user lies at the core of Maguire and Murray's ethos. Two further school buildings continue the same underlying ideas while also responding socially and topographically to their particular environments. North Crescent Primary School, Wickford, for instance, takes both *parti* (the dominating theme of the plan) and structural form from the Bow Common school and applies it to the suburban fringes of an Essex commuter town near Southend. Designed just after completion of the London school, it repeats the agricultural barn structure, in a setting close to actual countryside. The larger size of the site resulted in a decision to have a small 'barn' next to the main one, in which the assembly hall-cum-dining room and kitchen could be accommodated. This separation of activities hives off the smells and disturbance of school dinners, and gives greater scope for shared resource areas at the heart of the main building. In contrast to Bow Common, the mezzanine is given over completely to the children; it functions as an upper-deck teaching area, pure and simple, with three straight-flight staircases up to it, one from each teaching zone. The teachers' zone is located underneath, at the northern edge, with children's lavatories and audiovisual room occupying the remainder.

At Wickford, the eaves overhang by a generous 4 m depth to the east and west, with the gable front to the south overhanging to the same extent. On the north side of the building, by contrast, there is a trim gable end with no overhang. These projecting roofs give the school great presence within the site, but in a manner wholly consistent with the building's tectonic logic. The mezzanine deck engenders the feeling that the entire building is the children's domain; indeed 'deck' is entirely apt a word, as the 'funnel' which encases soil/vent pipes from the lavatories beneath further plays on the boat metaphor in an unforced but playful manner.

Children in the landscape

Maguire & Murray was an eminently meritocratic practice staffed by young, committed architects and students willing to pitch in and work long hours when required. Commissions were generally earned either in competition, or because of the high reputation gained through achieving prominence in certain areas of design. The commission that follows would be an exception to this pattern. It was a project which developed in the practice's new setting. In 1974 the lease on the office on Kew Green came up for renewal; the new rent had ballooned, owing to hyperinflation in the wake of the oil crisis following the 1973 Arab–Israeli conflict. The partners decided to find

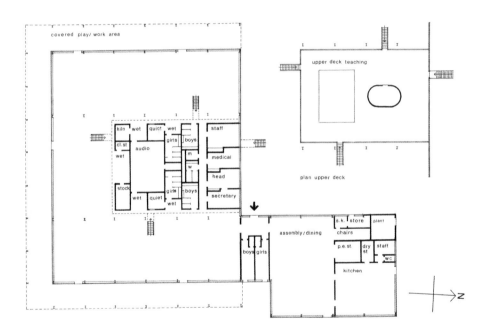

top: Wickford County Primary School, east-west section and south elevation
above: Wickford County Primary School, plan

top: Wickford County Primary School, Essex, interior
above: Wickford County Primary School, interior under construction

cheaper accommodation nearby at St John's Road, Richmond, the home of the practice until 1988.

Jake Nicholson's brother Andrew, whom Maguire had got to know in his early years at the AA, had become a governor of Claremont Fan Court School, Surrey. Following the Bow Common and Wickford schools, he put Maguire & Murray on the shortlist for a new building, which led to their commission for a new junior school. Here was a site steeped in architectural, as well as national, history. Claremont has an early landscape garden by Charles Bridgeman, a grand house by Capability Brown, and follies by John Vanbrugh. The young Princess Victoria spent much of her youth here before becoming Queen. Into this historic landscape Maguire and Murray planted a modest school.

The design for Claremont used a modified and refined rustic aesthetic. It stood in the same relationship to its predecessor schools as a seventeenth-century *sukiya*-style house might in relation to a plain Japanese farmhouse. The Japanese allusion is not whimsical, for the paired eaves brackets, the horizontal timber siding, generous, low-silled windows and high-level ridge glazing recall the many borrowings from the Japanese *sukiya* tradition by the architect Kazuo Shinohara in the 1960s and 1970s.

Gone is the open plan. Instead we have paired classrooms with communicating doors to enable team teaching to take place if desired. The two infant and two junior

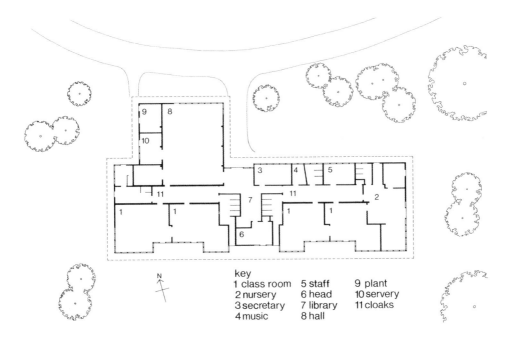

key
1 class room   5 staff   9 plant
2 nursery   6 head   10 servery
3 secretary   7 library   11 cloaks
4 music   8 hall

above: Claremont Fan Court Junior School, Surrey, plan

above: Claremont Fan Court Junior School, playground edge

classrooms open directly to the south, with doors in a continuously glazed facade giving onto a covered veranda. The much narrower building cross-section dictates that this is not as deep as those at Bow Common, or Wickford. The classrooms are accessed internally from both sides of the 'corridor', which is wide enough to accommodate all manner of shared resources. Most significantly, the corridor is not directly beneath the roof ridge, allowing the band of glazing in the ridge above to light the back of the classrooms as well as the corridor. This rooflight lends the building the character of a Victorian bathhouse, adding to its allure and helping it to fit within the special landscape. The entrance on the north side is formed by the right-angle of the protruding hall (accommodating dining room-cum-gymnasium) jutting out against the line of cellular rooms for staff.

Maguire and Murray also worked on buildings at King's School, Canterbury and Magdalen College, Oxford, but while these were significant projects, their importance lay more in their approach to aesthetics and conservation, rather than to the more strictly defined requirements of educational buildings.

In Germany

The *Internationale Bauausstellung* (IBA), a well-funded urban regeneration scheme for West Berlin involving many architectural practices, was one of the biggest architectural events of the 1980s. It came at the end of a line of twentieth-century exhibitions of housing that included the *Weissenhofsiedlung* in Stuttgart (1927) with its houses by J. J. P. Oud, Peter Behrens, Le Corbusier and Hans Scharoun, and *Interbau* 1957, which rebuilt the bombed-out Hansaviertel north of the Tiergarten in Berlin. The IBA had two purposes: the new projects, largely in the form of prestigious housing schemes and cultural buildings on vacant sites; and the 'critical reconstruction' of Kreuzberg, the inner-city working-class suburb to the south of the (original) city centre. This side of the IBA had a more radical, grass-roots nature, and often involved working with the original fabric. This was the side of the IBA that Maguire and Murray were engaged with.

IBA projects were initiated by limited competition and the Dutch architect Herman Hertzberger was tipped to win this one for a children's day centre. The site was on a vacant part of a housing block in southern Kreuzberg. A typical nineteenth-century inner Berlin housing block with grey-rendered fire-walls six storeys high hems it in to the north and the east; to the west is a communal garden of the neighbouring tenement block. To the south is the *Landwehrkanal*, a dreamy, almost bucolic tree-lined expanse of water, cut in the nineteenth century to aid barge navigation through Berlin. The project was for a kita, a *Kindertagesstätte* (children's day centre), a quasi-public provision of key importance in ameliorating the lives of children and their parents in Berlin. Kitas offer care for children in three age groups: from shortly after birth to three, from three to six (the official start of primary education), and from six to thirteen, offering facilities for afterschool activities for this age group, attending from 1.00 to 5.00 p.m. They were originally a feature of East Germany's extensive social

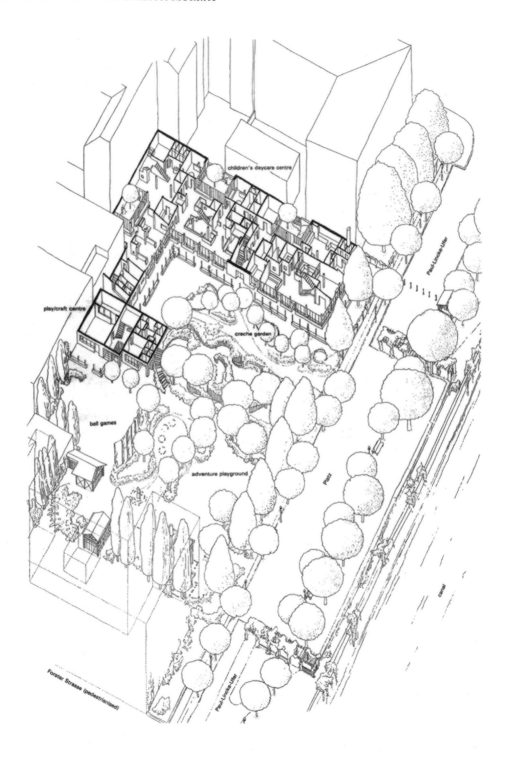

children's daycare centre

play/craft centre

creche garden

ball games

adventure playground

Platz

Paul-Lincke-Ufer

Paul-Lincke-Ufer

Canal

Forster Strasse (pedestrianised)

Paul-Lincke-Ufer

top: Kita, Berlin-Kreuzberg, interior
above: Kita, exterior from the southwest
opposite: Kita, cut-away isometric

provision, allowing both parents to work full-time. After 1968, radicals in West Berlin copied the idea which was taken up with alacrity, spreading thence to West Germany proper. Maguire and Murray were enchanted by this challenge: here was a pedagogic aim expressed by the users which chimed in so well with the ideas developed at the Bow Common school.

Kitas were generally laid out in a linear, cellular plan, the 'classrooms' progressing in age from youngest to oldest. Maguire and Murray's scheme retains this linear transition, but they sought to blur the edges between all but the very youngest groups of children by overlapping the zones, as if they were chain-linked Venn diagrams. The zones have subtle subspaces delineated by low walls as at Bow Common; in addition, intriguing child-scaled hideaways enliven the interior, customising each zone. Their aim was to make 'houses' of each zone, a feeling heightened by the two storeys, with domestic-scale staircases defining each section. What intrigues and delights is the fact that Maguire and Murray imported the very English idea of the two-storey house and reinterpreted it, with all its spatial richness, for children who invariably live in single-storey apartments, be they post-war flats or *Mietskasernen* ('rental barracks', or tenement blocks) which are the norm for Kreuzberg.

Their winning the competition surprised the practice and the local Berliners: everyone assumed the job would go to Hertzberger, who went on to build the acclaimed housing on Lindenstrasse, opposite the site where Daniel Libeskind's Jewish Museum was built some ten years later. Indeed the Dutch architect's approach was not dissimilar to that of Maguire and Murray, both practices being concerned with close observation of life, and of patterns of use. Indeed, Hertzberger's architecture had much of the kasbah about it. Getting this prestigious commission meant a great deal to the practice, and Maguire and Murray were determined that in its execution the kita should lose nothing of its design ethos and ambition. But they had never built abroad before, let alone in a city where the relationship of contractor to architect was subtly different in some important respects to practice in the UK. For instance, local building codes were more stringent, and the contractor assumed greater responsibility for detailing and specification than is the case in Britain.

A local architect, Joachim Schmidt, dealt with detailed negotiation over consents, and building contracts. One of his earliest problems concerned the 'loose' plan and section of the 'overlapping houses', because fire regulations stipulated far greater compartmentation. This was too difficult to sort out from the Richmond office, so Ekkehard Weisner, a German architect working for Maguire and Murray who had overseen the Lutheran Centre in London, was sent over to work directly with Schmidt for a period of three months. A compromise was thrashed out which retained the domestic character of the interior. The official insistence that lavatories should not be internal but must be naturally ventilated led to the introduction of two small court-yards against the rear party wall to the east, breaking up the relatively deep section, and introducing welcome spatial variety and natural light. The progression of 'houses', from crèche at the canal side through to infants, and finally juniors, remains a finely balanced resolution of community and privacy, demonstrating the detailed attention to the way buildings are used that was extolled by Serge Chermayeff and Christopher Alexander in *Community and Privacy*. At the northeast corner, where the linear progression has to turn through 90° in order to continue to the west, the greatest scale of interior volume occurs, with an almost Baroque staircase surmounted by a bridge structure for children to crawl along.

Nearly twenty-five years on, the kita is thriving. Its essential features have been well maintained, and although the space has been further subdivided, largely for reasons of sound isolation, the alterations have been sensitively executed. The stepped cross-section and pagoda-like piling up of pitched roofs help to diminish the scale of the building against its backdrop of sheer gable-end walls. The attached pitched-roof veranda running round the entire south- and west-facing edges brings the scale down to the level of the sandpits and playground furniture in the entrance courtyard. The scheme reinforced Maguire and Murray's reputation in German-speaking Europe, where they had already achieved good press coverage, and where Maguire had frequently lectured, although working overseas took its toll on the cohesion of the practice, and exacerbated the tensions between the partners.

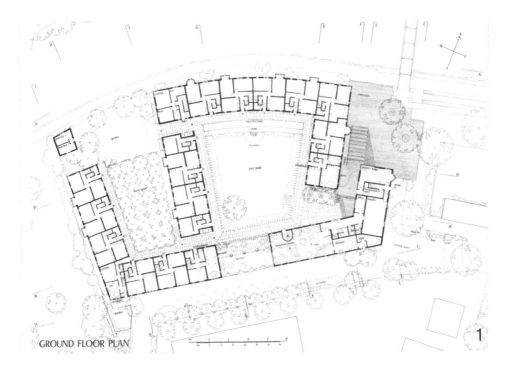

GROUND FLOOR PLAN

above: Pembroke College, Oxford, site and ground floor plan

Pembroke, Oxford

Maguire and Murray's scheme for Pembroke College, Oxford was one of the last by the original partnership. Pembroke is one of the smaller of the Oxford colleges and its only previous patronage of modern architecture was for Powell & Moya's small McGowin library of the 1970s. The College acquired a large piece of land on the banks of the Isis, a short walk from the main buildings, and a design competition was duly launched. As the only site to offer direct access to the river, it promised much from a picturesque perspective, despite problems of ground contamination from its use as a Victorian gasworks and of security from its remoteness. Maguire and Murray's scheme capitalised on the setting by proposing a prominent set of buildings acting as 'gateway to Oxford' from upstream and affording excellent views onto the river, while at the same time solving the poor site conditions and requirement for security at a stroke by raising the building up on a ventilated undercroft.

The brief asked for traditional sets of student rooms grouped around staircases, which Maguire and Murray designed with doors giving directly onto either of two

top: **Pembroke College, riverside entrance**

quads. The staircase groups create terraces of houses with two storeys of study bedrooms and a top attic floor of shared kitchens and sitting rooms nestling into the steeply pitched slate roof. In this sense the internal layout is similar to Stag Hill Court, and the later student housing for Jesus College, Oxford, where the usual arrangement of a house is turned on its head, so that private spaces are lower down, and communal rooms at the top. It is an ingenious plan, because the staircases to the attic storey reduce the institutional character by rising from a different point from the lower stairs, while the kitchen/dining spaces all have views over the river. Doors connect the adjacent top floors, allowing emergency escape and a discrete opportunity for the staircase groups to intermingle that is only 'understood' by the students themselves. It makes for an intriguing, rich mix of spaces and potential linkages.

The plan is linear, but bent and cut to fit the site and to offer the security that the College demanded. The entrance, consisting of a gate and porter's lodge, is formed in the slippage between parallel blocks. Because the whole building is raised up on its undercroft, the ground-floor windows look out to the river over the heads of passers-by

above: **Pembroke College, view over river**

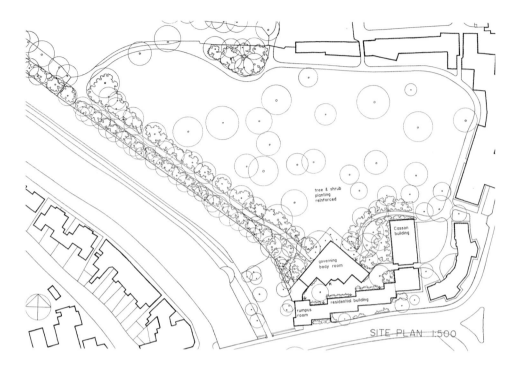

on the river walk below, and keep prying eyes away from the intimacies of College life. The two quads have very different characters. The larger of the two, with a sunken lawn, comes first, while the second has a dense, formal rose garden, originally conceived as an orchard. The scheme offers traditional comforts and the accustomed privacy of an Oxford college, with each of its different components of quads, houses, staircases and sets progressively more shielded and protected from the outside world. The College continues to value and praise the ingenious way these comforts were fashioned out of an unpropitious site. That it did so in an architectural language evoking the traditional Oxbridge college, and unmistakably suggestive of the Cotswolds, was viewed as a lapse, if not a transgression, by certain critics in the architectural world, prompting a debate that reflects more widely on British architecture in the last decades of the twentieth century.[9]

Exotic Worcester

Worcester College is an eighteenth-century foundation overlooking an extensive and well-planted landscape garden, including a tunnel between the garden and the entrance quad that Charles Dodgson, the fellow of Christchurch more famously known as Lewis Carroll, imagined as the rabbit hole in *Alice in Wonderland*. The problem was to insert

above: Worcester College, Oxford, site plan showing the curtailed Casson building and the garden restored

PERSPECTIVE: HYTHE BRIDGE STREET

top: Worcester College, view of roof of Governing Body room from loggia of Linbury Building
above: Worcester College, perspective

a relatively small amount of accommodation into the historic landscape, while still giving it sufficient presence and identity at the southward edge of its walled garden with a student residential building designed by Casson and Conder to the east. The area between this building and the line of the wall that separates the College from Hythe Bridge Street was the site of the new Linbury Building. The Casson and Conder block (1963) jutted unfortunately into the garden and the Linbury brief stipulated that it should be cut back.

The study bedrooms are unusually generous in size at around 20 m², including an *en suite* bathroom that makes them suitable for the conference trade. From the street the new buildings raise their heads above the wall, increasing in height in an echelon of four staggered blocks. The lowest of these blocks replaces the last section of the wall, giving the appearance that the whole building grows as the low-pitched, pyramid roofs rise, like organ-pipes, until they match the height of the Casson and Conder building. The basic layout consists of pairs of rooms accessible from a corner staircase in each of the blocks, with each staircase giving onto a loggia on the garden side to the north. There are loggias, too, at the top of three of the housing blocks, imparting an Italian feel to the scheme, as if it might be in Bologna. The use of coloured smooth and textured renders

above: Worcester College, view from Hythe Bridge Street

externally harmonises well with the stained oak window frames and the low-pitched zinc roofs. It is a cheaper specification than using natural stone for the walls; this compensated to some extent for the very generous room sizes. It also aids the reading of the building as an essay in the Italian Neo-Rationalism of Aldo Rossi, while the fact that the stone buildings of the Cotswolds would originally have had shelter coats of roughcast or limewash adds a further significance to this choice of materials. It is as if the nooks and crannies of the Pembroke buildings had been ironed out while the overall form is more articulated. The roofs have been reduced to a much lower pitch, while at the same time raised off their supporting walls and made to appear to float above their loggias. The building's appearance is both terribly familiar, with the Oxfordshire/ Cotswold detail of window sill flush with surrounding masonry and curiously exotic (Italy-cum-Japan) in the massing and form of the 'organ-pipe' elevation.

On the garden side the scheme finds its apotheosis in the Governing Body Room. This is a single-storey pavilion nestling in the trees, pulled away from the student accommodation to form a courtyard between, and rotated at 45° to the wall. To the Maguire and Murray aficionado it is a cross between the roof of the Church of the Ascension at Hulme and the Garden Room at Kew Green, a diminishing tower of

above: Worcester College, 'rumpus' room

square against larger square, each successive roof rotated 45° in relation to the roof below. In its detailing it is a hybrid of influences, from the Miesian cruciform steel columns to the deep shadows of the overhanging eaves, redolent of Frank Lloyd Wright's Robie House in Chicago. Despite the diversity of stylistic provenance, the buildings and spaces, internal and external, do nonetheless cohere. On the plan, the low form mentioned earlier that begins the sequence of rising towers contains what is described as a 'rumpus room', a novel concept for an Oxford college, but a better description than the conventional 'junior common room'. The neo-rationalist exterior conceals the homage to De Stijl within, where the murals recall Theo van Doesburg's dancehall of 1928 in the Café Aubette, Strasbourg. Worcester, a college with an exceptional archive of drawings by Sir Christopher Wren and other architects, can be proud of the fine collection of twentieth-century stylistic references represented in the Linbury Building.

Oxford School of Architecture

From the mid-1970s to the mid-1980s, Robert Maguire was Head of the Oxford School of Architecture (at Oxford Polytechnic, later Oxford Brookes University), arriving as a youthful, committed practitioner who was popular with students and staff. He abolished marks in first year in a bid to focus students' attention on the quality of their work, rather than chasing grades. He encouraged group working in the studios, a way of learning passed on from the AA in the early 1950s, and transformed the undergraduate first degree into a diagnostic one, intended to bring out the student's aptitude for architecture, while making entry to the Postgraduate Diploma course much more competitive.

By the time he retired from teaching in 1985 Maguire had made the Oxford School the strongest of the future '1992' universities created out of former polytechnics, and it has retained its reputation. The school provided the practice with a steady stream of young architects eager to begin professional life. Environmentally responsive architecture was a specialism of the school, reflecting Maguire's practical interest in developing modern design 'out of the "ordinary"', and complemented by his colleague Paul Oliver, the world expert on vernacular architecture as well as early American jazz.[10] Within four years of his retirement from Oxford, Maguire wound up Maguire & Murray, with both principals going their own ways. The story of the split is told in the final chapter; here the significant projects of Maguire's new enterprise, Maguire & Co, will be related as they invariably conform to the 'school' building type.

Master planning

In the 1980s, Maguire & Co were among the many British architects who looked for work overseas to make up for the lack of opportunities at home. Some of this was by competition, but the most significant schemes were direct commissions from Saudi

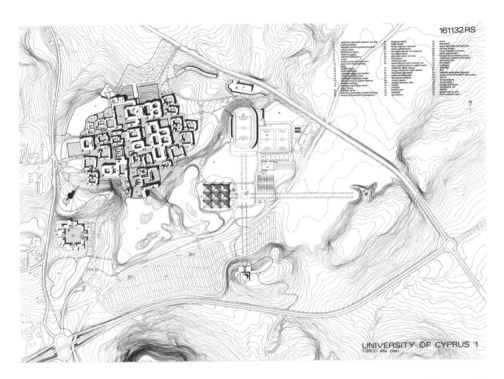

Arabia. In 1989 they were asked by their structural engineers Glynn Miller if they would be interested in taking over the design and execution of a large project in Buraydah. The Japanese architect Kenzo Tange had abandoned work on the scheme, and Maguire & Co were duly appointed. The work for King Saud University at Al Kassim campus encompassed a variety of buildings and led to a direct commission from the University, for its Abha campus in the Azir region. An ambitious master plan, never realised, was drawn up incorporating shaded pergolas along a pedestrian spine. There was a separate campus for women students with a string of paired courtyards containing accommodation in domestic flats. The library building was indicative of the practice's readiness to take suggestions from local design, with horizontally louvred elevations and patches of bright colour redolent of traditional construction in the region.

Although sadly unrealised, Maguire's competition entry for the master plan of the University of Cyprus scheme reached the finalist stage. Maguire & Co prepared the scheme in collaboration with Photiou Architects of Nicosia, the environmental consultant Dominic Michaelis, Ove Arup and Partners as engineers, and Colvin & Moggridge as landscape architects. In the arid rural landscape an agora was created: a formal, tree-shaded central square, with residential and academic courtyards spread out to the south in a vehicle-free environment. Nowhere in the whole complex is more

above: **University of Cyprus, landscape plan**

top: Master plan for the Abha Campus of the King Saud University, Saudi Arabia, model of women's residences

above: Abha – local inspiration (photo by Robert Maguire)

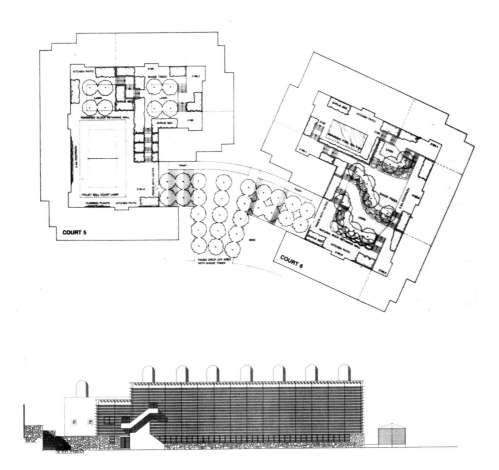

than ten minutes' walk from anywhere else, as Maguire's contention is that academic creativity depends on informal interaction over lunch and drinks. The residential court-yards incorporate everything learned by Maguire in his UK student housing schemes: a hierarchy of manageable groupings of five or six students sharing an apartment, then six apartments sharing a stair (two apartments per floor), then six or seven stairs grouped around a courtyard, and finally the dispersal of these courtyard buildings evenly around the site, with a noticeable 'grain' creating a network of major and minor paths. The Cyprus scheme was a collage of previous English projects, initially at Stag Hill, Guildford, and then at Pembroke and Worcester, Oxford, adapted for the fiercer eastern Mediterranean climate and larger scale of institution. The scheme makes eminent sense at whichever scale it is viewed, from the way individual students relate to their peers,

top: Abha Campus of the King Saud University, plan of women's residence courtyards
above: Abha Campus of the King Saud University, library elevation

to the way that the formal centre gives way to the informality of courtyard layouts the further we get from the centre, akin to the relationship between the orthogonal geometry of St Mark's Square in Venice and its more chaotic hinterland.

School geometry

Prior to his retirement from practice at the age of 72 in 2003, Maguire worked on two further schools in England. Dormston School, Dudley, a state comprehensive school in the West Midlands, had a disparate set of buildings, the most recent being a

above: Dormston School, Sedgley, looking down from the coffee bar and picture gallery onto the curved walls of the sculpture gallery
opposite: Dormston School, public entrance

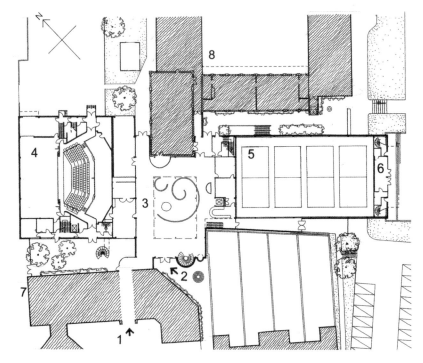

Theatre, art gallery and sports hall, Dormston School

KEY			
1	school entrance	3	foyer/ art gallery	6	pavilion
2	public entrance	4	theatre	7	existing arts building
		5	sports hall	8	existing school buildings

Postmodern Arts block which did little to make a coherent whole. Like many school sites, Dormston had grown piecemeal without an overall plan. The innovative aspect of Maguire's scheme lay less in its architecture than in its vision of a school embedded in its community, opening its facilities after school hours to its local residents. This was the premise on which funding for a new sports hall and theatre was based, and Maguire rose to the challenge, providing excellent facilities for both of these uses while bringing together the incoherent school layout at the same time.

top: Dormston School, Sedgeley, West Midlands, plan and section

A roof-glazed atrium served as the public entrance to the school, offering a foyer space to theatre and sports hall. It was a cool essay in white, with painted blockwork and a tubular steel roof structure, acting as a gallery space for art exhibitions, notable for a white constructivist spiralling wall. According to the critic Jeremy Melvin, the curves of this wall 'imply a miniature Corbusian interpretation of a small Mogul Indian observatory'.[11] An upstairs gallery, accessed by a white-painted steel spiral staircase set within a semicircular drum and overlooking this courtyard, leads to a small, top-lit alcove used as another exhibition space. With its common vocabulary of rounded forms, the atrium space resolves the jumble of conflicting buildings in a deceptively simple manner. For Maguire, it was a return to the aesthetics of *Circle*, the survey of 'International Constructive Art' edited by Naum Gabo, Leslie Martin and Ben Nicholson in 1937.[12] The diagonal relationships set up between vertical elements recall similar rotational geometries used at West Malling Abbey Church, and the rounded forms those at the Northolt church.

Radley College is a boys' boarding school established in the 1850s near Abingdon, not far from Oxford, based around Radley Hall, a country house of 1725. The house had suffered deterioration in plan and decorative treatment since the 1790s and was painstakingly restored in collaboration with Alison Maguire. The ground floor reception rooms were linked back together to make the enfilade with views through a sequence of doorways, typical of the period, while another axial view, passing from north to south through the centre of the house and known as the 'glide', was reinstated.

The Maguires shared a concern for the architectural integrity of buildings, whether historic or contemporary, and this informed the many church reorderings undertaken by the practice, while it also extended to an insistence on architectonic and spatial integrity in new work. In 1990 the practice had received the commission to convert a gymnasium at Epsom College, Surrey into a library. The generous volume of the lofty hall was retained, with lighter mezzanine galleries inserted. This pattern was followed in the conversion of a timber-framed barn at Radley into a library in 1996.

Two major new buildings both followed variations on a circular theme. Queen's Court (1995–97) was a two-storey 'doughnut' with a ring of classrooms and laboratories enclosing a serene courtyard. An overall roof with a central rooflight was considered at first, but this homage to a nineteenth-century railway roundhouse was abandoned for the more useful courtyard scheme that was executed. It obscured the rather gaunt science block from the 1930s, an essay in reinforced concrete in the manner of Owen Williams, unhappily disguised earlier, and a Postmodern craft and technology block.

Maguire & Co buildings of this period often had a thin roof edge sheltering a metallic outrigging of suspended galleries, a defining feature of their final building at Radley, the Sports Pavilion. Set on high ground at the edge of the sports field, this comprises changing rooms on the ground floor with a helical stair leading up to the first floor and offering uninterrupted views over the sports field through its continuous ring of full-height windows and doors. These give onto the terrace with its filigree balustrade, surrounding the entire drum. The exposed roof structure is an elegant 'umbrella'

top: Sports' Pavilion, Radley College, exterior
above: Sports' Pavilion, top floor reception room

design which is clearly separated from the heavier base of the superstructure below – a trope seen repeatedly in the practice's work. These were buildings with definite style which subsequent historians would not have too much trouble in identifying and classifying, with traits that make them recognisable. Work done subsequently at Radley by architects who had previously worked with Maguire show their respect for their *lieber Meister* (as Frank Lloyd Wright referred to Louis Sullivan).[13]

Notes

1   Andor Gomme and Alison Maguire, *Design and Plan in the Country House: from castle donjons to Palladian boxes*, New Haven and London: Yale University Press, 2008, p.1.

2   Finmere school was designed by David and Mary Medd, with Pat Tindale of the Architects and Building Branch of the Ministry of Education. See Andrew Saint, *Towards a Social Architecture: the role of school-building on post-war England*, New Haven and London: Yale University Press; 1987, pp.188–190, and 'Chapter 28: Primary School

Buildings and Equipment' in *(The Plowden Report: 1967) Children and their Primary Schools. A Report of the Central Advisory Council for Education (England)*, London: Her Majesty's Stationery Office, 1967, pp.395–396.

3   Eveline Lowe School was designed by David and Mary Medd of the DES Development Group. The main job architects were John Kay and Norman Reuter with GLC architects for the ILEA. See Andrew Saint, *Towards a Social Architecture: the role of school-building on post-war England*, New Haven

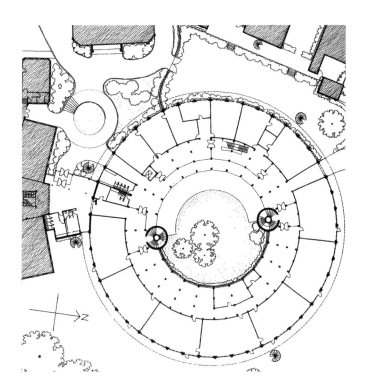

top: Queen's Court, Radley College, Abingdon, ground floor plan, laboratories, classrooms, and subject-club spaces

and London: Yale University Press; 1987, pp.192–193, and 'Chapter 28: Primary School Buildings and Equipment' in *(The Plowden Report: 1967) Children and their Primary Schools. A Report of the Central Advisory Council for Education (England)*, London: Her Majesty's Stationery Office, 1967, p.400.

4 ibid., p.400.

5 Maguire in conversation with the author, 17 March 2011.

6 This apt characterisation was included in an email to the author from Robin Bishop, 4 March 2011.

7 Jeff Bishop, 'School at Bow Common, Building Appraisal', Architects' Journal, 9 August 1972, p.314.

8 Comments made by Robert Maguire in conversation with the author, 22 November 2009.

9 See Peter Blundell Jones's review of the competition entries, including an assessment of Maguire & Murray's winning scheme, Peter Blundell Jones, 'College collage', *Architects' Journal*, 11 June 1986, pp.29–49.

10 'Something out of the "ordinary"' was the title of Maguire's keynote lecture at the RIBA annual conference in Hull in July 1976. Paul Oliver was the founder of the International Vernacular Architecture Unit at the Oxford School of Architecture, author of *Dwellings: the house across the world*, Oxford: Phaidon; 1987, and editor of *Encyclopedia of Vernacular Architecture of the World*, Cambridge: Cambridge University Press; 1997. The foreword written by Maguire for the *'Humanes Bauen'* exhibition catalogue includes 'Five Lessons'. These are reprinted here as an appendix, and do much to explain – and correct misunderstandings of – Maguire's relationship to 'the vernacular'.

11 Jeremy Melvin, 'Heart of class', *RIBA Journal*, May 2001, p.42.

12 Leslie Martin, Ben Nicholson and Naum Gabo (eds), *Circle: international survey of constructive art*, London: Faber & Faber, 1937.

13 David Welbourne of GBS Architects designed the theatre at Radley, completed in 2005.

above: Queen's Court, Radley College, Abingdon, courtyard
opposite: Queen's Court, exterior

5   Style

The history of art is no longer the history of styles. The notion of style, which once seemed to define the discipline, has loosened its grasp on our thoughts about art; many of the most powerful minds of the field have subjected it to critique; it is not adequate to our thinking about visual form and representation today.[1]

Frederic J. Schwartz, *Blind Spots*, 2005.

Maguire and Murray had a clear sense of where they belonged stylistically, both having had a solid grounding in architectural and design history. For them, the development of architecture was no longer a matter of a 'succession of styles'; social function and symbolic meaning were what mattered. As they wrote in 1965, 'The social function of architecture was a constant theme of most of the founders of the Modern Movement in architecture; it reversed the generally accepted nineteenth-century concept of architecture as an art in which style is paramount.'[2] Style was a dangerous concept since it introduced extraneous considerations that tended to decouple designers from their clients. '[Should] architecture become[s] a matter of style, the relationship between client and architect is of little consequence. But once the architect recognises that a building fulfils a practical and symbolic function in the life of a community then this relationship becomes crucial. The architect must get in touch with the life he serves.'[3]

Maguire and Murray shared the view of the Arts and Crafts architects that buildings had a 'practical and symbolic' function, the expression of which resided in appropriate construction and, on occasion, careful decoration. The need for the latter was one well expressed by Keith Murray who maintained:

> *There is a need for decoration which has been repressed by conformity to Modern Movement dogma. To respond to this need, it is necessary to distinguish the essential social inspiration of the Modern Movement in architecture from its stylistic manifestations, freeing ourselves from puritan inhibitions, so that decorative arts in relation to buildings can, in [William] Morris's words, be 'born again'. Perhaps doing crafts like pottery, boat building, weaving and jewellery, could help to develop our skill of head and hand. If then we can add the quality of heart by breaking down the barriers which separate creator and user, a fully humane architecture could arise which includes but goes beyond the utilitarian.[4]*

Keith Murray wrote these words in the *Architectural Review* in the mid-1970s, in a decade of acknowledged blight in British design, where the certainties of taste of mid-century, and of belief in rational progress as the saviour of mankind of the 1960s,

opposite: Oxford University Club, Oxford, galleries facing the playing field

were followed by a descent into architectural mediocrity and ideological uncertainty. His aim was to equate appropriate decoration in buildings with the renewed search for ornament in studio pottery in the 1950s. He went on to defend two Maguire & Murray buildings from the 1960s that were criticised for their applied decoration, namely the 'olde-worlde' leaded lights at West Malling Abbey, and the 'Cosmati' patterning to the quad pavement at Trinity College, Oxford.

Certainly, the oil crisis of 1973 had thrown all assumptions about material wellbeing and sustainability into disarray. Murray's response to this was an inward search for the roots of modern design, a return to craftsmanship – even to the decorative arts – that might once again realign architecture with authentic traditions of manufacture. Murray proposed a view of the psychological and social function of decoration akin to that of Christopher Alexander, as expressed in Alexander's books, *The Timeless Way of Building* and *A Pattern Language*. While Maguire was influenced by Alexander's earlier collaboration with Serge Chermayeff in *Community and Privacy*, a book that recommended courtyard houses, so Murray would find common ground with his subsequent notions of 'patterns' – elements of design from a wide range of periods and places, ranging from urban concepts to domestic lifestyle suggestions, among which simple forms of decoration were encouraged. In the same article Murray cited the Suprematist artist Kasimir Malevich: 'As in nature, so in the creations of man there exists an urge to create form (whether utilitarian or not), to decorate, to give it an artistic, beautiful appearance.'[5] Maguire & Murray's architecture based on need – of the client, and of the craftspeople making the building – caused them to be characterised, together with architects like Edward Cullinan and Walter Segal, and Jim Johnson of ASSIST in Glasgow, as new kinds of architectural heroes. The architect-anarchist Colin Ward grouped these radical voices together, finding them sympathetic because 'It is the way they go about their work which excites rather than the formal qualities of their finished buildings.'[6]

Maguire and Murray's version of Modernism was perhaps closest to that strand of Nikolaus Pevsner's *Pioneers of Modern Design*, 1949, that charts the English Arts and Crafts with its notions of propriety, economy and honesty as being one of the components of the Modern Movement. For them, architecture as a social art certainly had an ethical purpose, expressed through authentic and appropriate deployment of materials. The concerns of the Modern Movement, like those of Morris and Lethaby, were not primarily concerned with 'style' as an exercise purely based on visual aesthetics, devoid of any social, constructional or functional basis. In this sense Maguire and Murray's allegiances and sensibilities were more aligned to the ethos of the New Brutalists than to the purely visual interests of the Festival of Britain style, or its successor, dubbed 'contemporary' by design historians.[7] Here is Maguire (with close friends from the Architectural Association) writing a letter to *The Times* in 1950 (reprinted in an article by Nikolaus Pevsner, 'Canons of criticism', in the *Architectural Review* in January 1951) attacking what for them were Sir Giles Gilbert Scott's antiquated views of architecture obsessed with 'style':

> *style is a visual quality associated with architecture quite unrelated to the*
> *spirit and techniques of the time, and in which it is perfectly possible to design*
> *power house chimneys in the manner of Greek temple columns, telephone*
> *kiosks with the fenestration of eighteenth-century villas, and a new Parliament*
> *building as a Tudor manor house. … In any great period architecture evolves*
> *out of contemporary thought and method of building, fulfilling the needs of*
> *the time and creating its own forms. It must do the same to-day even if some*
> *members of the profession are content to mark time.*[8]

Maguire and Murray would concur with the art historian Frederic Schwartz that
'the history of art is no longer the history of styles.'[9] 'Style' was certainly anathema to
Maguire, as it was for many Modernists of his generation. For them the Postmodernist
moment in British architecture, from the late 1970s throughout the following decade,
remains a bleak episode in design history. In many respects the best work of such
practitioners had already been achieved, and the blight of pediments, curlicues and
other applied baubles was for them an undignified coda in the development of architecture. Yet the vocabulary of style remains a useful shorthand for professionals
and lay people in order to characterise a building's appearance. Osbert Lancaster's
'Stockbrokers' Tudor' immediately – and conveniently – summons up faux timber-
framing, while 'Moderne' connotes streamlined, white-rendered buildings from the
interwar period of the twentieth century.[10] The point is that these soubriquets are
generally used pejoratively by informed critics and practitioners, and innocently and
in good faith by the untutored public. In the latter case, they tend to denote (external)
features of buildings to the exclusion of the 'style' of the building's construction or
layout, so that when a contemporary house is described as 'Georgian', it will have a
raised and fielded front door with fanlight above, or more ignorantly incorporated, but
may not have planning and other features intrinsic to an eighteenth-century house,
such as coal fires, sculleries and servants' quarters in the attics.

'Astragal', the gossip column in the *Architects' Journal*, made the first attribution of a
homage to Maguire's style in 1961 when it reported that

> *Robert Maguire's attempts to give liturgical planning a convincing architec-*
> *tural form got a stormy reception, but his views on top lighting and glazed*
> *lanterns have prevailed. The Church of the Holy Rood, Folly Bridge, Oxford,*
> *above, is the first of the Sons of St. Paul's, Bow Common in that respect, if in*
> *no other.*[11]

This Roman Catholic church at well-named Folly Bridge was designed by an architect-
admirer of Maguire's who had got to know his work through the New Churches
Research Group, and who had latched onto some of Bow Common's more obvious
superficial features. This was a back-handed compliment to Maguire, who was more
bemused than annoyed at having been plagiarised in this manner. Yet despite many
modern architects' unease with style as a label when it is applied to their own work,
it is nonetheless a commonplace that original designers and artists should have the
superficial traits of their work copied: witness the displays of muscular concrete and

random windows in the wake of the publication of Le Corbusier's church at Ronchamp in the mid-1950s, or the rash of Accrington red brick and patent glazing once Stirling and Gowan's 'red' university buildings of the 1960s had been written up. Alan Berman, who worked with Maguire and Murray in the 1980s, maintains that '[these buildings'] "style", the "taste" or the "appearance" (plain terms which [Berman uses] intentionally to include the participation of non-architects) may be strange, difficult to comprehend, or even unattractive, is to say nothing other than that comprehension is necessarily difficult in any language that is unfamiliar.'[12] Berman is attempting to bring back the word 'style' and to show that it still has a useful role to play in the public – and professional – understanding of architecture; in doing so, he defuses the charged, confrontational meaning of the word and makes it, once again, acceptable in polite architectural company.

Romantic Pragmatism

In three projects from the mid-1970s to the 1980s Maguire and Murray demonstrated their skill at working with historic buildings. During these decades, conservation, including the insertion of new buildings into historic settings, became a major concern among architects and commentators, and several firms with a reputation for original work surprised themselves and others by showing their adaptability and sensitivity in this new role, which required them to find forms of expression sympathetic to the past but not directly imitative of it. Maguire and Murray, separately and jointly, had recognised the importance of context, be it physical, social or psychological; even their new buildings and artefacts arose from a deep consideration of these various contexts, and their design invariably originated from various sources. Most of their work for the Church, for instance, was concerned with reordering existing layouts, and their new work would be unthinkable without this background knowledge and skill. Their most famous early works, such as St Paul's church and school, and the student housing at Surrey, answered the need to create a new context rather than to respond to an existing one, but they soon showed themselves adept at the demanding task of fitting in. In a celebrated article in the *Architectural Review* in September 1983, Gillian Darley and Peter Davey included Maguire and Murray under the umbrella of 'Romantic Pragmatism', a tag they shared with other architects such as Cullinan, MacCormac Jamieson Pritchard, Aldington Craig & Collinge and Ralph Erskine. Darley and Davey wrote,

> It celebrates the primacy of the individual and particular and, pragmatically, it responds to the exigencies of brief and site without introducing … an irrelevant geometric discipline between programme and product. Because of its direct response to circumstance, need and surrounding, Romantic Pragmatism is informed by tradition but it is not eclectic. It is gentle but not weak. It is responsive but not kitsch. It is systematic – indeed it inherits much Modern Movement thinking – but it is not severe. Romantic Pragmatism is essentially regional. It suggests multifarious ways

in which people who use buildings can identify with locality, with particular
places. The individual and small group become generator and focus of archi-
tectural effort. Romantic Pragmatism is one of the most potent, multivalent
and liberating approaches to architecture today.[13]

Kenneth Frampton's influential essay on 'critical regionalism' was published in the same
year, making a suggestion that a 'third way' was already evident by which the various
forms of alienation produced by Modernism could be tempered without surrendering
its strengths and virtues.[14]

Maguire's first-year student report '8 Districts' from 1949 showed his early understanding of the dilemma in which 'progress' could appear destructive of local identity.
Maguire noted that the post-war shortage of stone and stonemasons was coupled with
the cheapness and ready availability of brick throughout the country. For him, 'This
means that the character of many parts of the country will change. What is more: as
the gradual mechanisation of building technique develops, the character will change
further still.'[15] However, rather than regarding these changes as necessarily deleterious
to the art of building, Maguire believed that, if handled sensitively and intelligently,
unavoidable changes could lead to a renewal of the modernist spirit:

It need not change for the worse. As this survey [of the vernacular building
traditions of eight rural regions] shows, character is formed by men using
the materials and methods available, in a direct and convenient manner
to fulfil their requirements. It is not decided arbitrarily. We can create
a valid character as long as we continue to use available methods and
materials in this way. The Georgians altered the character of London in a
valid manner. The between-war speculative builder did not. What is to be

above: '8 Districts' report, drawing of farm buildings in Norfolk, Robert Maguire, 1949

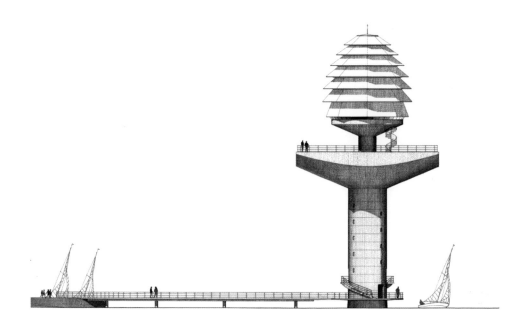

avoided is not so much the loss of present character, but the formation of
an invalid new one.[16]

Their practice was pragmatic, then, in its willingness to use currently available
materials and methods, but romantic, too, in its implicit search for aesthetic validity
in both history (local building traditions) and theory (the impersonal rules and conditions underpinning recognised styles such as the Georgian). What is telling, in the
buildings designed by Maguire and Murray through the 1960s and 1970s, is their
continuation of an English Arts and Crafts ethos, with the admixture of developments
pragmatic and aesthetic derived from modern architecture as it developed through the
twentieth century. A competition drawing of Maguire's from 1968 for a Carillon Tower
at Canberra, Australia is pure 1960s in its hopeful trust in contemporary 'engineered'
forms while appearing solid and timeless in its simply sculpted shaft and 'capital'.
Murray recognised this in his article 'Concern for the craft', from 1976, in which he
stated,

> *There is a reaction to the sterility of ... Modern Movement dogmatism which*
> *could result either in a positive development of the reforming zeal for life*
> *inherent in the movement or into an unmitigatedly reactionary ornamental*
> *bandwagon, either historical-eclectic or modern, which the various*
> *machining and moulding technologies are admirably adapted to exploit.*[17]

above: Carillon Tower, Canberra, Australia, elevation, 1968

Learning from the vernacular

By the middle of the 1970s, architecture in Britain had reached its nadir, as popular dislike of the products of modernism, based on both technical failure (such as with the block of flats at Ronan Point, East London, 1968) and aesthetic doubts (1976 saw the completion of both the National Theatre designed by Denys Lasdun, and the Pompidou Centre, Paris, designed by Renzo Piano & Richard Rogers). In October 1976 the *Architects' Journal* ran a long, navel-gazing study of the plight of British architecture, while in West Germany an exhibition at Bielefeld entitled *Humanes Bauen* (humane building) showcased Maguire & Murray as offering a way out of the morass of technocratic, unfeeling building.[18] The projects exhibited in Bielefeld, including the Bow Common school, the Stag Hill student housing and West Malling abbey, suggest how architecture might escape the impasse by paying close attention to user–client needs, physical context, and being attuned to the pragmatics of the building industry. If the client body lacked a unified view, even the most sincere architects could not achieve their best results, as Maguire and Murray discovered with St Joseph's Church, Northolt, completed in 1970. Maguire has recently pondered its problems:

> While the plan, structure and detailing are all some of the most sophisticated I think I've ever done, I feel the church has a sort of coldness about it, the cause of which I'm well aware of. The parish consisted of two housing estates, one pre- and one post-war, on opposite sides of a busy dual carriageway. There were intrinsic resentments between the two, never overt but which one felt very strongly during any discussion with the PCC or Building Committee. This made it impossible to 'get close' to the parish, as we had done at Crewe [All Saints Church, 1962–7]. It was all wordy with no feeling, and so we were left to our own devices as to what sort of building to design. The result is elegant but cold.[19]

With its scheme for Magdalen College, Oxford the practice returned to form. Despite being won in competition (1975), with all the associated problems of lack of briefing and meaningful dialogue with the client (including, most importantly, the user-clients), the scheme emerged as clear winner from the field of 144 entries. The scheme represented a classic case of architectural 'problem-solving', then a popular phrase. The College had a wonderful medieval kitchen, a lofty atmospheric place at ground level but difficult to reach from the first-floor Hall. Maguire & Murray's scheme rebuilt the working kitchen at first-floor level, finding a site for it in the entrance yard where a covered delivery bay was created beneath, shielded by the conserved wall of the old bathhouse that fronts the river, and facing Magdalen Bridge, the site of undergraduate pranks on May Morning. The old kitchen was converted into the College bar, with an array of intimate rooms leading off it, and giving onto a new river terrace, private to the College. The new kitchen replicates the cross-section of the old one with a high, lofty ceiling beneath a pitched roof detailed externally to match the medieval character of Magdalen.

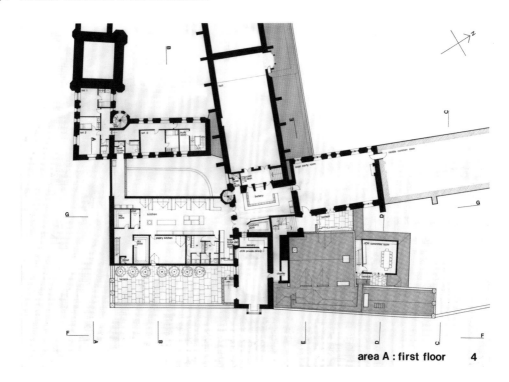

area A : first floor   4

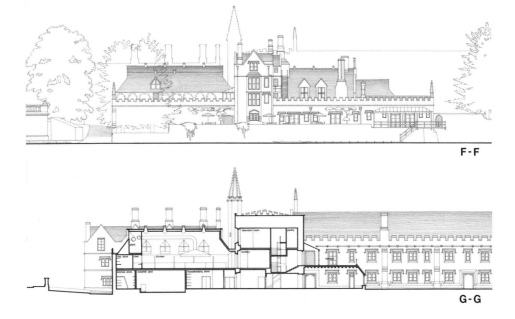

F - F

G - G

top: Magdalen College, Oxford, plan of competition entry 1975, largely realised in the 1980s
above: Magdalen College, river (east) elevation and section

King's School, Canterbury gave Maguire and Murray a similarly precious architectural context. The brief asked for accommodation for day students and boarders, as well as laboratories and an extension to the dining hall, all of which were skilfully fitted into the school enclave within the cathedral precinct. The client had originally thought that any new building would have to be located outside the walled precinct, on a site some fifteen minutes' walk from the main school premises. Maguire and Murray argued that for the sake of maintaining the school community the accommodation had to be within the walls. After investigating the site and looking at the historic record, their conviction increased, for they discovered that ancient fabric had been demolished in the nineteenth century in order to open up the Precinct to afford grander views of the Cathedral. By redensifying the plan through the insertion of appropriately scaled buildings, Maguire and Murray aimed to reinforce the pre-Victorian 'grain' of the Precinct. In many respects this kind of archaeological approach was akin, if opposite in effect, to their reordering of churches where they sought to retrieve the medieval openness of the church interior by removing post-medieval organs, screens and furniture, allowing physical and spatial freedom for modern worship.

above: Magdalen College, view from High Street: the gablet of the new kitchen appears above the eighteenth-century castellations

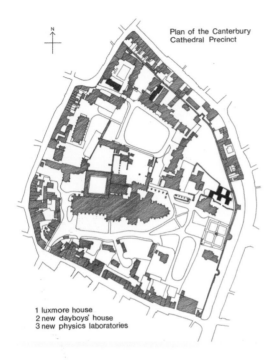

1 luxmore house
2 new dayboys' house
3 new physics laboratories

top: The King's School, Canterbury, Kent, location of new buildings (in black) in the cathedral precinct
above: King's School, Mitchinson's House, view from north

The scheme comprises three elements: the extension to Galpin's refectory, Luxmoore boarders' house and Mitchinson's building for day students. Luxmoore is hard by the Precinct wall and comprises five 'houses', groupings of study bedrooms strung along an east–west axis of common areas and staircases. Roofs dominate: great sweeps of red clay-tile, interrupted by simple, large dormer windows with triangular gables sheltering two storeys of banded blockwork walling. Collections of V-plan oriel windows hang down below the deep eaves in ones, twos or threes, an idiosyncratic detail that recalls the work of Philip Webb or Norman Shaw. Luxmoore has a precise and careful play of geometry in three dimensions, laid out with five 'hit and miss' fingers of dormitories to maximise the students' exposure to natural light and private external space.

The prominent position of Mitchinson's, located at one of the gates to the Precinct, called for a more nuanced distinction of scale and effect. It replaces the original barbican removed by the Victorians with a simple rectangular-plan block and a tutor's house at the west (city) end and study rooms double-banked off central corridors. The long south elevation, the 'outside', has greater variety of scale than the more sedate composed north elevation. As at Luxmoore, large triangular dormers punctuate the

above: **King's School, Luxmore House**

sweep of red-tiled roof, and on the south facade this extends right down to just above head height at the small-scale Romanesque gatehouse end. The north elevation has greater formality, with the roof edge extending down to the window-heads to the first storey. These windows run in a continuous horizontal band along half the length of the building, recalling the top-floor windows at the Lutheran Centre in London. The walls here are rendered, with a clock-tower forming the 'book-end' to the run of eaves windows to the east, an aesthetic owing much to the English Arts and Crafts, crossed with a touch of Charles Rennie Mackintosh.

The addition to Galpin's comprises a two-storey block shoehorned into a tiny space behind the main refectory, normal to it. On the ground floor is a physics lab, with the dining room extension above. This picks up a strong Kentish theme, with white painted timber weatherboarding to the south elevation. The dining room – used as the staff refectory – has 'bird box' light fittings similar to those designed for All Saints Church, Crewe. The room has excellent natural lighting, with its clerestory windows on the north face supplementing the generous south glazing, shaded by virtue of giving onto a tight narrow courtyard.

The work of Maguire & Murray in the 1980s, and the subsequent output of Maguire & Co through the next two decades, was at the forefront of the strain in British architecture which, while disdaining the excesses of Postmodernism, sought to counter the public's disenchantment with contemporary architecture. In his essay, 'The quality of simplicity' in 1983, Maguire argued that 'To be organic [a design] must be sensitive to the existing attributes of its occupants' way of life. While this is possible, there is a great temptation when using the vernacular to attempt the apparently "accidental" effects of long-existing places: this can give the disturbing impression of people living in a film-set.'[20] The 'Romantic Pragmatism' label of 1983 was an attempt to differentiate a continuation of a valid strain of Modernism from an unthinking rash of 'neo-vernacular' schemes which spread over the country in the wake of the Essex Design Guide in 1973.[21] It seemed by the mid-1980s as if any proposal for a new building with a pitched, tiled roof with the odd tower, gable or dormer would pass muster for planning approval. When the Maguire and Murray schemes did have these attributes, this was owing to the essentially domestic nature of the accommodation required, and they remained a questioning and critical practice.

Scenography in context

Chepstow Castle Visitors' Centre (1986–89) is a remarkably sensitive and witty scheme, self-effacing in its invisibility at the edge of the car park below the castle. Its 'tadpole' form of crinkle-crankle stone walls conceals 'servant' zones within spaces carved out of the apparent thickness of masonry. The interior is surprisingly expansive and is rooflit by a series of 'bicycle wheel' skylights, a device of Maguire's worked up by structural engineer Mark Whitby. The design is a departure on the part of Maguire. It lacks the clear, prismatic application of building materials that characterises all of the earlier

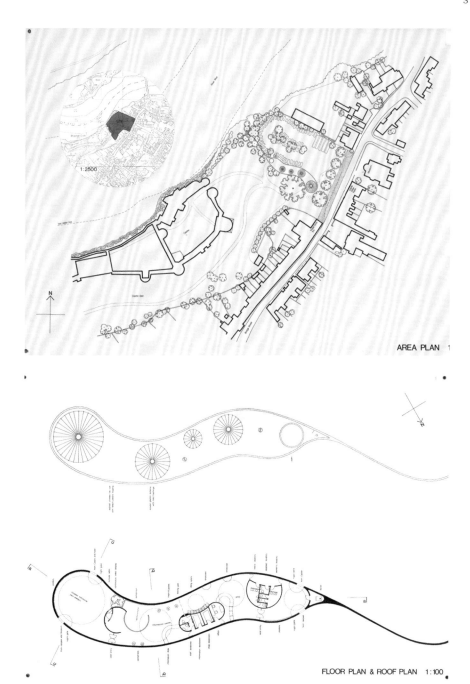

AREA PLAN 1

FLOOR PLAN & ROOF PLAN 1:100

top: Chepstow Castle Visitors' Centre, Monmouthshire, location and site plan
above: Chepstow Castle Visitors' Centre, floor and roof plans

work of the partnership with Murray while displaying a well-judged scenographic character, which makes it perfectly at ease in its setting, and clearly subservient to the castle to which it is an adjunct. It is an example of a 'blob' building before the term had come into general circulation, with its amoebic forms as freestanding peas (housing lavatories and other ancillary spaces) inside the pod-like external form, predating the library at Cottbus, Germany, designed by Herzog & De Meuron, by some twenty years.

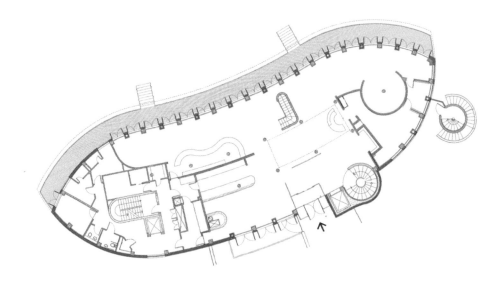

top: Oxford University Club, Oxford, upper ground floor plan
above: Oxford University Club, view from playing field

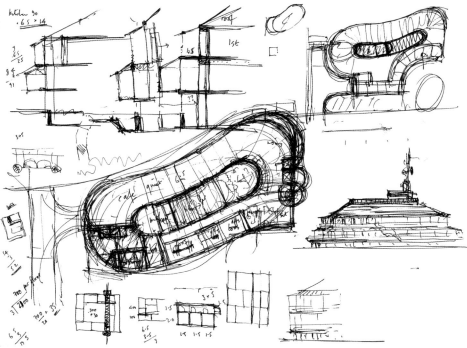

top: Oxford University Club, entrance front on Mansfield Road
above: Oxford University Club, early sketches

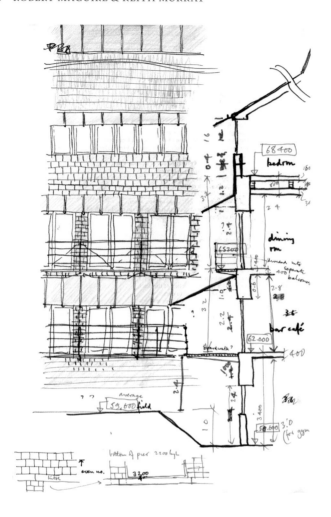

At the end of the century the Oxford University Club, one of the last buildings
designed under the Maguire & Co flag, reiterates the 'peas in a pod' motif of Chepstow.
The curiosity of the building, true to its description, is that it only has two elevations.
Two towers containing stairs and a lift shaft protrude from the outside edge, marking
the 'front' door, while the entire sports field facade acts as a grandstand facilitated by
lightweight metal balconies.

An unexecuted project from 1987, an invited competition scheme for the British
Ambassador's Residence in Moscow, proposed a villa heavily influenced not only by its
Russian context, but also by the British Arts and Crafts – 'Voyseyesque', according to
one critic.[22] The roofs dominate, hipped and double-pitched, with dormers and venti-

above: Oxford University Club, Maguire's section and elevational study, with final modular layout of
blockwork and all vertical dimensions resolved

lating cupolas cut into them. Borrowing from Luxmoore House at the King's School, Canterbury, the villa has many V-shaped oriel windows dropping down from the deep eaves. An influence from Moscow is the low pitch of the copper roofs, their concealed gutters allowing a sharp, crisp eaves detail, seen later at the Oxford University Club and Radley College.

Professional vicissitudes

As with so many of the projects, stringent site constraints at the University Club, together with financial constraints, were the starting point. It was one of the few examples of a commission won by the practice by fee bidding, to which Maguire was fundamentally opposed. The liberalisation of markets under the premiership of Margaret Thatcher had introduced this competitive element to the procurement of buildings in the wake of the abolition of mandatory fee scales by the RIBA in 1982 and architects were expected to tender competitively for their fees. Maguire has characterised the new ethos: 'all architects do the same thing; some are cheaper than others, so find the cheapest' rather than 'all architects work for the same fee; some are better than others, so find the best architect' which had hitherto prevailed.[23]

The other tendency was to loosen the architect's control over the administration of building contracts. For instance, quantity surveyors tended now to be nominated by the client, often over the heads of architects, resulting in weaker relationships within the building team. Maguire had a similar objection to the RIBA's revised competition system in the UK, believing it to be a cynical means of obliging architects to work gratis in the distant hope of being awarded a commission, even though Maguire & Murray, and Maguire & Co, did win many competitions. What rankled was the tendency of the competition system to elicit an eye-catching motif bearing little relationship to the client's actual needs. The way competitions were set up in the UK tended to cut out any meaningful contribution from the users, an aspect that both Maguire and Murray felt was important to getting a good result. The competition system in West Germany, where entries were subject to objective specialist and client scrutiny in addition to the more subjective juries comprising architects, was preferable. Maguire's ironic initial 'advice' in an article of 1982 to anyone contemplating entering an architectural competition was 'If you are not prepared to remember at every stage that your objective is to win the competition rather than design the best building for the users' needs, don't enter.'[24] The weariness reflects Maguire's suspicion of the influence that Charles Jencks's version of Postmodernism was having on the British architectural scene.

Maguire was also prescient about the coming transformation of the architect into a purveyor of images of buildings above all, rather than a provider of useful environments. When Maguire reviewed the Sainsbury Wing of the National Gallery, London in 1991, he wrote, 'All buildings speak. They do not need symbols imposed on them from other languages to do this. This building should surely have affirmed reality and spoken of the joy of seeing these wonderful pictures. Alas, it does not.'[25] During the

1980s, several UK schools of architecture, especially the Architectural Association in London then led by the ebullient Canadian, Alvin Boyarsky, were beginning to turn out exquisite drawings which were hard to relate to conventional notions of buildings.[26]

Departures and new beginnings

When in 1976 Maguire accepted the headship at the Oxford School of Architecture he knew it would mean being away from the office at Richmond for as many as three days every week in term time, but his keen interest in architectural education, combined with the prestige and additional income persuaded him to accept the challenge. The new arrangements left Murray in sole charge of the Richmond office whenever Maguire was away at Oxford. The routine of driving between Richmond and Oxford several times a week, often late at night, was punishing and in 1978 Maguire decided to move to Oxfordshire, to the village of South Weston, just off the M40 motorway. In 1986 the partners took the decision to open a second office at Thame, close to Oxford which further exacerbated a split in the office, with about half of the original staff staying on with Murray at the Richmond office, and some new staff recruited for Thame.

At the same time the kita competition success in Berlin was also taking its toll. Murray was the partner most involved with the project's eventual execution, and his frequent visits to Berlin during that phase brought him into close contact – and friendship – with Joachim Schmidt, their executive architect. Murray and Schmidt

above: Adolf-Damaschke-School, Berlin-Kreuzberg, main block showing raised roof

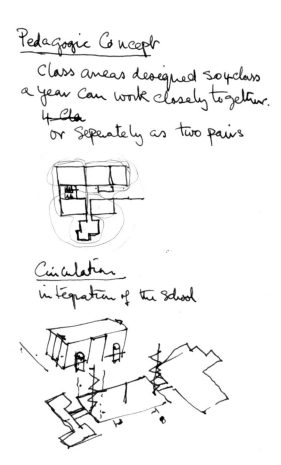

Pedagogic Concept

Class areas designed so class
a year can work closely together.
4 Cla
or Seperately as two pairs

Circulation
integration of the school

decided privately to work together on a number of Berlin projects, independently of Maguire back in England. The first resulted in another competition win for an IBA project to reorganise and extend a nineteenth-century school in Kreuzberg, a short walk north from the kita on Paul-Lincke-Ufer. Three more projects followed, although all suffered as a result of German reunification after 1989, when public funds were diverted to rebuilding in the former DDR.

In 1985 Maguire retired from his headship at the Oxford School due to overwork, and in 1988 both principals decided formally to end their partnership as a result of insuperable difficulties.[27] Although Maguire initially continued the new practice of Maguire & Co at both locations, the Richmond office was wound up in the 1990s recession.[28] Murray pursued his partnership with Schmidt, commuting between London and Berlin. By 1985 the kita project had already been completed.

above: **Adolf-Damaschke-School, Keith Murray, sketch of massing and planning**

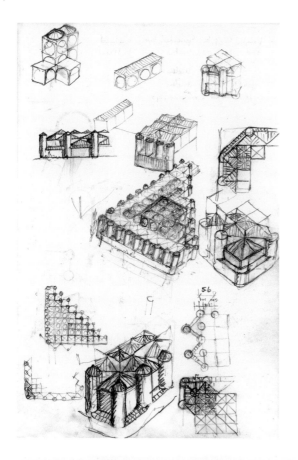

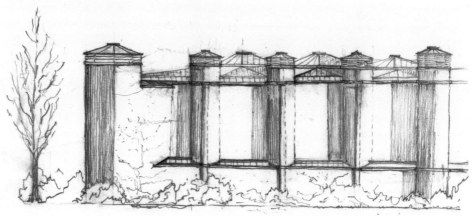

above: Jewish Museum competition, Berlin, Keith Murray, elevational compositional and massing studies

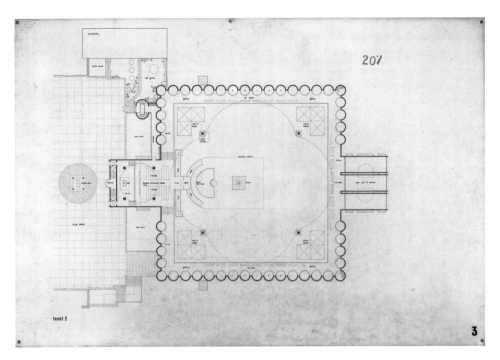

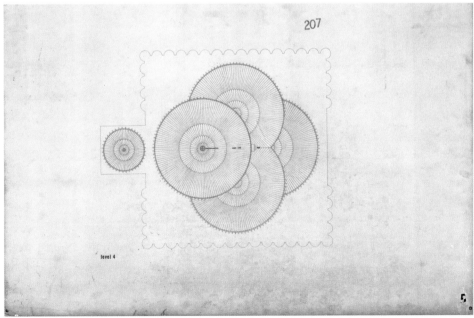

top and above: Liverpool Cathedral (RC) competition scheme, gallery and roof plans, Robert Maguire &
Keith Murray, 1961

Schmidt and Murray's scheme for the Adolf Damaschke Schule involved a building in the rear courtyard of a typical Berlin urban block structure on a large scale, hiding substantial civic and industrial buildings. They made the most of the siting of the four-storey, Prussian clinker-built school, placing towers of richly textured brick to the southeast of the main block and helping to break up and individualise the large surrounding courtyard space. Glass pergolas linked dispersed parts of the plan. The major intervention to the fabric of the solid school block was to raise the roof so that it appeared to hover over the deep shadow of a new clerestory window wrapping round the top of the whole building, bringing light to the attic storey. An intriguing sketch-scheme from 1988 – found in his sketchbook from that time – was Murray's (unsubmitted) response to the open competition for the extension to the (West) Berlin Museum to provide it with a dedicated department for Jewish history. This was won the following year by the architect Daniel Libeskind, becoming the stand-alone Jewish Museum. Murray's scheme derives from motifs of Byzantine architecture, and is an essay in repeat units of drums and cubes, a tectonically based scheme, a cross between Louis Kahn and Friedrich Gilly/ Karl Friedrich Schinkel. It also reiterates many aspects of the Maguire & Murray competition entry (1961) for Liverpool (RC) Cathedral.

above: **Madonna and child sculpture for St Mary's church, Lewisham, Keith Murray, 2004**

Murray resumed some UK design work after Schmidt's unexpected death at the end of the 1980s, collaborating with various architects on reordering churches and other historic buildings. The last project he completed was the wittily inventive extension and redesign of a wholefood shop in Kew, just around the corner from the Fabyc community. His last design, completed after his death in 2005, was a Madonna and Child sculpture for St Mary's Church, Lewisham, London.

Coda

In many ways the collaboration of Maguire and Murray was exemplary for architectural practice in post-war Britain. Schooled in the late 1940s and early 1950s, both Maguire and Murray had complementary qualities that suited them well in their subsequent partnership. Both were idealistic, both sought to combine their own highly practical skills with poetic flights of imagination. Their careers spanned the resurgence of British architecture in the post-war period, through the economic boom of the 1960s and through to the bust of the 1970s. By 1975, British architecture had reached a low point, in terms of both the profession's own self-esteem and its acceptance by the public. John Carter, in the *Architects' Journal* pessimistic *tour d'horizon* of the state of British architecture in 1975, wrote

> How could such transparently good and altruistic social aims [of the period
> 1945–55] lead us – apparently – into such trouble? How could the noble,
> humane ideals of the Modern Movement come so seriously unstuck? ...
> Technology and education were the means, and culture – if one can use
> the word in its common but distorted sense – was the eventual aim. Among
> the intelligentsia ... the possibility of a scientific culture was considered: a
> sort of scientific intellectual discipline with humanist values. Two things
> about these ideas should be noted: they offered no serious criticism of the
> nineteenth century's belief in 'progress' and they are entirely secular, ration-
> alist and materialist.[29]

Maguire and Murray's work escapes this condemnation. There are certainly aspects, such as the rational use of materials, the mastery of components, the familiarity with contractual processes, which belong to this image of the technocratic architect's belief in relentless progress, but these were balanced by their deeply felt social critique, their sense of the numinous and their understanding that the life which architecture is called on to serve is ultimately more important than the building itself. Above all they were practitioners, generally serving clients who had little money but plenty of ambition for buildings to provide the appropriate setting for modes of life, in addition to a representation of that life. Their disciplined buildings, frequently at odds with the meretricious mores of the 1980s and 1990s, have at last found an echo among British architects such as Adam Caruso and Peter St John, David Lea, Tony Fretton, Andrew Houlton, Stephen Taylor, Jonathan Sergison and Stephen Bates, all unafraid to work with received forms of recognisable building forms and familiar materials. In a wider context, this form of

architecture is part of what the Swiss architect and historian Martin Steinmann refers to as offering '*forme forte*', an antidote to shape for shape's sake that typifies much of twenty-first century design.[30]

Afterword

I have been lucky to have been able to speak to Robert Maguire on many occasions, to have had access to his archive, and thus to have gained valuable insights into the motivation behind his architecture. It is natural, in a partnership of two equals, to attempt to ascribe divergent traits and attributes to the two sides; people have sometimes tried to characterise Maguire as the rational, and Murray the romantic. Yet as the paintings, writings and readings show, a simplistic split is hard to justify. Indeed, Alexandra Harris in her book *Romantic Moderns* makes the point that Britain was particularly well placed to offer a synthesis of the individual, idiosyncratic and topographical with the logical, rational and pragmatic. She begins her study with a photograph by John Piper of a powerful, archaic carved Anglo-Saxon font from a church in Dorset; I end with a photo found in one of the cardboard boxes of Keith Murray's archive, a black and white study of an elaborately carved Norman font from St Mary's Church, Stottesdon, Shropshire.[31]

above left: Robert Maguire in his retirement in the Scottish Borders, where he has returned to abstract sculpture
above right: Keith Murray in the 1980s

top: 'Poise', Robert Maguire, 2010
above right: Teapot design, Keith Murray
left: Sketch of Humphrey Lyttelton playing the trumpet,
Keith Murray, 1955

The photograph is dated 1929 – the year of Murray's birth – and is likely to have been taken by his artist-mother. In the same cardboard box were his sketchbooks, including a study of Humphrey Lyttelton blowing his trumpet. The 900 years from Norman England to mid-twentieth-century bohemian Soho inform the wide and complex range of Keith Murray and Robert Maguire, and explain something of their significance for contemporary design. 'He made ordinary things special' are the words carved on Murray's tombstone, designed by Ralph Beyer, a sentiment that might be applied to both Robert Maguire and Keith Murray's long involvement with architecture, as well as to their individual contributions to contemporary life.[32]

> *The places that we have known belong now only to the little world of space on which we map them for our own convenience. None of them was ever more than a thin slice, held between the contiguous impressions that composed our life at that time; a remembrance of a particular form is but regret for a particular moment; and houses, roads, avenues are as fugitive, alas, as the years.*[33]
>
> Marcel Proust, *A Remembrance of Things Past: Swann's Way*, 1913.

above: Norman font, St Mary's Church, Stottesdon, Shropshire

Notes

1   Frederic J. Schwartz, *Blind Spots: critical theory and the history of art in twentieth-century Germany*, New Haven and London: Yale University Press, 2005, p.1.

2   Robert Maguire and Keith Murray, *Modern Churches of the World*, London: Studio Vista and New York: Dutton, 1965, p.14.

3   ibid., p.14.

4   Keith Murray, 'Concern for the Craft', *Architectural Review*, October 1976, p.206.

5   ibid., p.206, citing Camilla Gray's translation, Catalogue of Malevich, Whitechapel Art Gallery, London, 1959.

6   Colin Ward, 'Accidental heroes', *New Society*, 8 May 1978, p.374.

7   See Lesley Jackson, *'Contemporary': architecture and interiors of the 1950s*, London: Phaidon, 1994.

8   Letter dated 10 October 1950 from Michael Brawne, Alan Graham, Robert Maguire and Peter Matthews to *The Times*, published 13 October 1950, p.5, reprinted in Nikolaus Pevsner, 'Canons of criticism', *Architectural Review*, January 1951, p.6.

9   Frederic J. Schwartz, loc. cit., p.1.

10 Osbert Lancaster, *Homes Sweet Homes*, London: John Murray, 1939.

11 'Astragal', *Architects' Journal*, 6 April 1961, p.489. The architect was Gilbert Flavel.

12 Alan Berman (ed.), *Jim Stirling and the Red Trilogy: three radical buildings*, London: Frances Lincoln, 2010, p.146.

13 Gillian Darley and Peter Davey, 'Sense and sensibility', *Architectural Review*, September 1983, pp.23–25.

14 Kenneth Frampton, 'Towards a Critical Regionalism: six points for an architecture of resistance', in *Anti-Aesthetic: essays on postmodern culture*, Hal Foster, (ed.), Seattle: Bay Press, 1983.

15 Robert Maguire, '8 Districts: a survey of the traditional uses of local materials and the formation of local architectural character in eight districts in England and Wales', *Howard Colls Travelling Studentship*, Architectural Association: London, 1949 (unpublished report).

16 ibid.

17 Keith Murray, 'Concern for the craft', *Architectural Review*, October 1976, p.205.

18 John Carter, 'To endless years the same?', *Architects' Journal*, 6 October 1976, pp.630–661, and *Humanes Bauen*, exh. cat., Ulrich Weisner, (ed.), Kunsthalle Bielefeld, 15 June–3 August 1975.

19 Robert Maguire, 'Notes on projects', 2010 (unpublished).

20 Robert Maguire, 'The quality of simplicity', *The Fibrecement Review*, ac107, April 1983, p.5.

21 *Design Guide for Residential Areas*, Essex County Council, 1973.

22 Colin Amery, 'Embassy fronts classical intrigue', *Financial Times*, 5 December 1988. The title refers to the winning design by the architect Julian Bicknell.

23 See Linda Sandino, interviewer, 'National Life Stories Collection': British Library, 2004.

24 Robert Maguire, 'A service to the profession?', *Architects' Journal*, 29 September 1982, p.43.

25 Robert Maguire, 'Frontis' review, *RIBA Journal*, September 1991, p.12. The Sainsbury Wing, National Gallery, London, 1991, was designed by Venturi, Scott Brown and Associates, Inc. in association with Sheppard Robson Architects.

26 See Andrew Higgott, *Mediating Modernism: architectural cultures in Britain*, Abingdon: Routledge, 2007. (See in particular 'Chapter 6: Searching for the subject: Alvin Boyarsky and the Architectural Association School', pp.153–188.)

27 Maguire being honoured with the OBE in 1983, and Murray's partnership with Schmidt being splashed across the UK press with *Building Design* reporting their IBA win with the Adolf Damaschke School (27 July 1984) did little to improve an already tense relationship.

28 The Thame office was located initially at 30 High Street, moving to No. 104 in 1988.

29 John Carter, op. cit., 1976.

30 Martin Steinmann, *Forme forte: Ecrits/ Schriften 1972–2002*, Basel, Boston and Berlin: Birkhäuser, 2003.

31 Alexandra Harris, *Romantic Moderns*, London: Thames & Hudson, 2010, pp.7–9.

32 Ralph Beyer was too ill to carry out the work himself. The letters were cut by Peter Foster of Wattlington, Oxon.

33 Marcel Proust, *A Remembrance of Things Past: Swann's Way*, London: Chatto & Windus, 1957, p.288, trans. C. K. Scott Moncrieff.

List of Works

The following list provides a guide to all the buildings and selected projects undertaken by Keith Murray and Robert Maguire in their individual capacities, the practice of Robert Maguire & Keith Murray, and Maguire & Co. The list of works has been arranged chronologically and includes selected published references, awards, journals, competitions and unexecuted projects. A double asterisk (**) indicates that the project has been demolished. A single asterisk (*) indicates that it has been drastically altered, sometimes beyond recognition.

Chronological list of selected projects (years of design inception and project completion):

Keith Murray (with Michael Murray)

1954
Fit-out of chapel, St Katherine's Foundation*
Butcher Row, Tower Hamlets, London
(chapel designed by architect Roderic Enthoven in 1951; competition design by Michael Murray and Keith Murray; drawings by Robert Maguire)

Robert Maguire

1950
Exhibition stand for Crittall Metal Windows**
(competition design: with Michael Brawne, Michael Cain and Peter Matthews)
Olympia, London
Client: Crittall Metal Windows
First premium

1954
'Vita et Pax' chapel for the Monastery of Christ the King
Bramley Road, Cockfosters, Middlesex
(unexecuted project)
Client: Dom Joseph Brennan OSB, Prior

opposite: Magdalen College, Oxford, new kitchen seen form Magdalen bridge

1955
Kiosk for International Travellers' Aid**
Victoria Station, London
Client: International Travellers' Aid

1955–8
External restoration of the Round House
Havering-atte-Bower, Romford, Essex (listed Grade II)
Client: Mr & Mrs E. Heap

1955–60
St Paul's Church, Bow Common
St Paul's Way, Bow Common, Tower Hamlets, London
Client: The Vicar and Parochial Church Council of St Paul's
(Keith Murray, under his artistic pseudonym, Keith Fendall, received the commission for the mosaics; Charles Lutyens took over this work and brought it to completion, basing his final design on Murray's scheme.)
Listed grade II*
Edward D. Mills, *The Modern Church*, London, Architectural Press, 1956, p.138
Architectural Review, April 1958, p.255
Peter Hammond, *Liturgy and Architecture*, London, Barrie & Rockliff, 1960, pp.111–14
Architectural Review, December 1960, pp.400–5
Peter Hammond, (ed.), *Towards a Church*

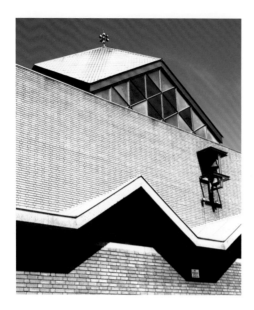

St Paul's, Bow Common, view of bell and roofs

Architecture, London, Architectural Press, 1962, pp.154–8
Småkirkebladet, Oslo, May 1962, pp.3–7
Churchbuilding, October 1962, pp.14–24
Reyner Banham, *Guide to Modern Architecture*, London, Architectural Press, 1962, p.27
Sam Lambert, *New Architecture of London*, London, British Travel & Holidays Association, 1963, pp.76–7
Ian Nairn, *Modern Buildings in London*, London, London Transport, 1964, p.25
Robert Maguire & Keith Murray, *Modern Churches of the World*, London, Dutton Vista, 1965, pp.90–93
Ian Nairn, *Nairn's London*, Harmondsworth, Penguin, 1966, pp.164–5
Architects' Journal, 8 July 1970, p.70
Christliche Kunstblätter, Linz, February 1970, pp.61–2
Edwin Heathcote & Iona Spens, *Church Builders*, London, Academy, 1997, pp.68–73
Elain Harwood, contributor, *The Twentieth Century Church*, London, Twentieth Century Society, 1998, pp.69–71

1957–60

House (for Colin and Rosemary Boyne)
Kentlands, Hildenborough, Kent
Client: Mr and Mrs D.A.C.A. Boyne

1957

Remodelling of showroom for Watts & Co**
Dacre Street, Westminster, London
Client: Watts & Co.
Showroom dismantled after Watts & Co. relocated

1958

Competition entry for Ipswich Civic Centre
(in collaboration with Peter Whiteley: unexecuted project)
Client: Ipswich Borough Council
Commendation

1958–60

Reordering of the east end of Pershore Abbey
Pershore, Worcestershire
Client: The Rector and Parochial Church Council of Pershore Abbey
Status: reordering of rest of church carried out beautifully in 1990s by Michael Rearden

Robert Maguire and Keith Murray

1959–63

St Matthew's Church, Perry Beeches
Aldridge Road, Perry Beeches, Birmingham
Client: The Vicar and Parochial Church Council of St Matthew's
Listed grade II
Peter Hammond, (ed.), *Towards a Church Architecture*, London, Architectural Press, 1960, pp.159–60
Birmingham Post, November 1964
Observer Weekend Review, 31 January 1965
Architects' Journal, 6 October 1965, pp.793–802

Architectural Review, October 1965, pp.250–1
Country Life Annual, 1967, pp.50–1
Nikolaus Pevsner & Alexandra Wedgwood,
The Buildings of England: Warwickshire,
Harmondsworth, Penguin, 1966, p.196
Christliche Kunstblätter, Linz, February 1970,
pp.61, 83
Edwin Heathcote & Iona Spens, *Church Builders*,
London, Academy, 1997, pp.68–73
Church Building, March–April 1998, pp.65–7
Elain Harwood, contributor, *The Twentieth
Century Church*, London, Twentieth Century
Society, 1998, pp.72–3

1959–60
Refurbishment of Staff Social Club at
Warlingham Park Hospital
Warlingham, Surrey
Client: The Staff Social Club

1959–62
Conversion of St Lawrence's church hall to
a church (RC)
High Street, Edenbridge, Kent
Client: The Revd Fr O'Sullivan

1959–66
Cumberbatch Quadrangles at Trinity
College and Blackwell's Norrington Room
bookshop
Broad Street, Oxford
Clients: Trinity College, Oxford and BH
Blackwell Ltd
Oxford Magazine, Summer 1966, pp.439–1
The Bookseller, 18 June 1966, pp.2550–2
Illustrated London News, 25 June 1966, p.15
Architectural Review, November 1966,
pp.338–48, and May 1967, pp.361–3
Status: bookshop has undergone several subse-
quent refits

1960
Competition entry for Liverpool Roman
Catholic Cathedral
Liverpool
(unexecuted project)
Client: The Roman Catholic Archdiocese of
Liverpool

1960
Landscaping at Wexham Springs Research
Centre
Wexham, Slough, Buckinghamshire
Client: Cement and Concrete Association

1961–2
Reordering of the east end of St Andrew's
Church, Old Headington*
Headington, Oxford
Client: The Vicar and Parochial Church Council
of St Andrew's
Status: Subsequent reordering by others has
reversed much of the simplicity of this scheme

Norrington Room – interior showing bookshelving
system

1961–2

Temporary exhibition of Rubens's Adoration of the Magi in the ante-chapel of King's College Chapel

Cambridge

Client: King's College, Cambridge

1961–3

Extension and reordering of St Mark's Church, Smethwick

Londonderry, Smethwick, West Midlands

Client: The Vicar and Parochial Church Council of St Mark's

1961–3

Fabyc House residential conversions and extensions

Cumberland Road, Kew Gardens, Surrey

Client: The Fabyc Housing Association

1962

Reordering of the east end of King's College Chapel

Cambridge

(unexecuted project)

Client: King's College, Cambridge

Apollo, May 2004

1962–4

Reordering of St Thomas's Church, Heptonstall*

Heptonstall, Hebden Bridge, West Yorkshire

Client: The Vicar and Parochial Church Council of St Thomas's

Nikolaus Pevsner & Enid Radcliffe, *The Buildings of England: Yorkshire West Riding*, Harmondsworth, Penguin, 1967 edition, p.631

Status: major additions to the furnishings and organ have since been made

1962–6

New monastic church, cloister, living accommodation and landscaping at St Mary's Abbey, West Malling*

(additions to a group of ancient buildings)

West Malling, Kent

Client: The Benedictine Community of St Mary's Abbey

The Abbey Church is listed grade II*

Architectural Review, November 1966, pp.338–42

John Newman, *The Buildings of England: West Kent & the Weald*, Harmondsworth, Penguin 1969, pp.576–7

Concrete Quarterly, January–March 1969 and September 1975, pp.31–4

Daily Telegraph, 17 May 1969

The Architect, January 1973, pp.39–41

Financial Times, 27 December 1975

Edwin Heathcote & Iona Spens, *Church Builders*, London, Academy 1997, pp.68–73

Building Design, 26 February 1999

Church Building, May/June 1999, pp.62–3

Cloister & Living Accommodation listed Grade II

Status: the only significant change to the scheme as designed and executed is the introduction of columns in the church for structural reasons.

1962–7

All Saints Church, Crewe

Stewart Street, Crewe, Cheshire

Client: The Vicar and Parochial Church Council of All Saints

Architects' Journal, 4 September 1968, pp.453–64

Christliche Kunstblätter, Linz, No. 2 1970, p.61 and pp.78–82

Nikolaus Pevsner & Edward Hubbard, *The Buildings of England: Cheshire*, Harmondsworth, Penguin 1971, pp.187–8

Edwin Heathcote & Iona Spens, *Church Builders*, London, Academy 1997, pp.68–73

1963

St Thomas's Church, Cherry Hinton

(unexecuted project)

Cherry Hinton, Cambridge

Client: The Vicar and Parochial Church Council
of St Thomas's

Nicholas Taylor, *Cambridge New Architecture*,
Cambridge, Trinity Hall, 1964, p.57

1963

**Demountable nave sanctuary at Worcester
Cathedral**

Worcester

Client: The Dean and chapter of Worcester

1963–6

The Church of the Redeemer, Tye Green

Tye Green, Harlow

Client: The Evangelical Lutheran Church

1964

Extensions to St Teilo's Priory (C of E)

Cardiff

(unexecuted project)

Client: Community of the Resurrection

1964–5

**Reordering of the chapel of the Hostel of
the Resurrection***

Leeds, West Yorkshire

Client: The Community of the Resurrection

Status: the chapel is now the Common Room of a
students' residence

1964–6

St Luke's Church, Scawthorpe

Scawthorpe, Doncaster, South Yorkshire

Client: The Vicar and Parochial Church Council
of St Luke's

Nikolaus Pevsner & Enid Radcliffe, *The
Buildings of England: Yorkshire West Riding*,
Harmondsworth, Penguin 1967 edn, p.623

1965–6

**Reordering of the chapel of St Michael's
Convent**

Ham Common, Surrey

Client: The Community of St Michael's (C of E)

1965–8

**Rebuilding of Marriott House, with art
bookshop for Blackwell's**

(part of Grade II listed group)

Broad Street, Oxford

Client: Trinity College, Oxford & BH Blackwell
Ltd

1966

**Reordering of St Helen's and St Katherine's
school chapel**

Abingdon, Oxon.

Client: St Helen's and St Katherine's school

1966

Reordering of St Andrew's Church

(unexecuted)

Shifnal, Salop

Client: The Vicar and Parochial Church Council
of St Andrew's

1966

Reordering of St Michael's Church

(unexecuted)

Malton, Yorks.

Client: The Vicar and Parochial Church Council
of St Michael's

1966

Reordering of St Benet's Chapel

Queen Mary College, Mile End, London.

Client: Queen Mary College

1966

Conversion of stables to Lutheran Church and Community Centre**

Sunbury, Middlesex

Client: The Evangelical Lutheran Church

Status: Demolished

1966–7

Conversion of house to flats for the elderly

Bushwood Road, Kew Gardens, Surrey

Client: The Mary Orchard Housing Association

1965–70

Church of St Joseph the Worker, Northolt*

Yeading Lane, Northolt, Middlesex

Client: The Vicar and Parochial Church Council of St Joseph's

Architects' Journal, 8 July 1970, pp.69–84

Lance Wright, 'Manplan 5: Religion', *Architectural Review* March 1970, pp.205–8

1967

Riding School

(unexecuted)

Kirtlington, Oxon.

Client: unrecorded

1967–9

Remodelling of Mowbray's bookshop

Margaret Street, Marylebone, London

Client: AR Mowbray Ltd

1967–70

Stag Hill Court, student housing at the University of Surrey

Guildford, Surrey

Client: The University of Surrey

Architects' Journal, 17 March 1971, pp.585–600

RIBA Journal, April 1971, pp.140–8

Times Educational Supplement, 25 June 1971

Concrete Quarterly, April–September 1971, pp.2–9

Design Magazine, September 1971

Daily Telegraph, 6 November 1971

William Mullins & Phillis Allen, *Student Housing: Architectural and Social Aspects*, Crosby Lockwood, 1971

AC Review, Zurich, January 1972, pp.7–13, and April 1976, pp.12–15

Baumeister, Munich, October 1972, pp.1124–7

Entwurf und Planung, Munich 1973

George Perkin, *Housing, Landscape and Concrete*, Cement and Concrete Association 1975, pp.24–5

1968

Invited competition entry for a carillon tower as UK's gift to Australia, on Canberra's Jubilee

(unexecuted project)

Client: The Foreign and Commonwealth Office

1968–9

Refitting of bookshop

St Aldate's, Oxford

Client: AR Mowbray Ltd

1969–70

Garden room and landscaping

Kew, Surrey

Client: Mr & Mrs Bruce OB Williams

1969–71

St John's Theological College

Bramcote, Nottingham

Client: St John's College (formerly The London College of Divinity)

Building Design, 15 October 1971, p.14

Architects' Journal, 20 October 1971, pp.846–7

AC Review, Zurich, October 1974, pp.14–16

Art d'Eglise, Ottignies, January/March 1975, pp.213–19

George Perkin, *Housing, Landscape and Concrete*, Cement and Concrete Association 1975, pp.8–9

Status: a chapel and library have been added by others

1969–71

New vestries and reordering of St Leonard's Church, Wollaton

Wollaton, Nottingham

Client: The vicar and Parochial Church Council of St Leonard's

1969–71

St Paul's with St Luke JMI School*

Bow Common, Tower Hamlets, London

Client: The Diocese of London (C of E)

The Observer Review, November 1971

Design Magazine, April 1972, pp.48–54

Architects' Journal, 9 August 1972, pp.309–24

Education, October 1973, pp.437–9

Baumeister, Munich, October 1973

1969–72

Church of the Ascension, Hulme*

Hulme, Manchester

Client: The Vicar and Parochial Church Council of the Ascension

Status: various alterations have been made, including the glazing of the gallery

1970–1

Conversion of house to flats, and landscaping

Broomfield Road, Kew Gardens, Surrey

Clients: Mr & Mrs George Mason

1970–2 and later phases

Upgrading of the clubhouse of the Oxford and Cambridge University Club

(Grade I listed building by Sir Robert Smirke)

Pall Mall, London

Client: The Oxford and Cambridge University Club

1971–3

St Peter's Church, Didcot

Didcot, Oxfordshire

Keith Murray, silver jug and bowl, mid-1960s.

Client: The Vicar and Parochial Church Council of St Peter's

Illustrated London News, November 1977

Kunst und Kirche, Linz, March 1982, pp.148–9

1971–4

Students' Union building at the University of Surrey*

Guildford, Surrey

Client: The University of Surrey

Architectural Association Annual Review, October 1977

Status: much changed by ad hoc additions and fundamental redecoration

1971–6

East Slope Student Housing at the University of Sussex*

Falmer, Sussex

Client: The University of Sussex

Status: appearance radically changed by replacement windows

1972
Reordering of St Saviour's Church
Stamshaw, Portsmouth
Client: The Vicar and Parochial Church Council
of St Saviour's

1972–3
Reordering of the chapel at Quarr Abbey
Near Ryde, Isle of White
Client: The Benedictine Community of Quarr
(RC)

1972–4
Wickford County Junior School
Wickford, Essex
Client: Essex County Council
AC Review, Zurich, October 1976, pp.10–12
Education Supplement, 26 November 1976, p xi
'Education' School Design Awards:
commendation

1972–4
**Court 5 Student Housing at the University
of Surrey**
Guildford, Surrey
Client: The University of Surrey

1972–6
St Augustine's Roman Catholic Church
Calverey Park, Tunbridge Wells, Kent
Client: The Rev W Howell
Clergy Review, January 1978, pp.37–40
Kunst und Kirche, Linz, 1982, pp.145–7

1973
Student Hotel
London (unexecuted project)
Client: International Student Travel Association

1973
**Conversion of the Oxford Union Society
building to a students' club**
Oxford (unexecuted project)
Client: The Oxford Union Society (in collabo-
ration with International Student Travel
Association)

1973–4
**Sports changing rooms and groundsman's
facilities**
Richmond, Surrey
Client: The London Borough of Richmond upon
Thames

1973–5
Shared Church, Brighton Hill*
Brighton Hill, Basingstoke, Hampshire
Clients: Local Anglican, Methodist and Roman
Catholic church authorities
Status: with many ad hoc additions, the building
is now unrecognisable

1974–8
**The Lutheran Centre: Student Hostel,
Church & Chaplaincy**
Bloomsbury, London
Client: The Lutheran Council of Great Britain (in
collaboration with the British Council)
Architects' Journal, 4 April 1979 pp.665, 668–71,
and 3 October 1979, pp.703–17
Baumeister, Munich, November 1980,
pp.1097–1102
Kunst und Kirche, Linz, March 1982, pp.150–2
Civic Trust Awards 1979

1975–7
**Houses for married students at St Stephen's
House, Oxford**
Norham Gardens, Oxford
Client: St Stephen's House
Architects' Journal, 25 January 1978, pp.159–170
AC Review, Zurich, October 1979, pp.26–8

1975–8
Guy Harlings conference centre and diocesan offices
Chelmsford, Essex
Client: St Albans & Chelmsford Church Trust
(C of E)
Civic Trust Awards 1980

1975–8
Claremont Fan Court Junior and Nursery Schools
Claremont, Esher, Surrey
Client: The Claremont Fan Court Foundation
Ltd
RIBA Journal, March 1981, pp.44–5

1975–85
Demountable nave sanctuary and choirstalls, interior refurbishment and rebuilding of the ceremonial West Steps at St George's Chapel, Windsor Castle
Windsor, Berkshire
Client: The Dean and Chapter of Windsor
Report of the Society of Friends of St George's,
1981–82, pp.98–108
Crafts, September/October 1979, p.9

1975 and 1986–8
Extensions and refurbishment at Magdalen College, Oxford
Oxford
Client: Magdalen College (1975 and 1986–88)
Architects' Journal, 30 April 1975, pp.900–6
Financial Times, 12 May 1975
Limited Edition, Oxford, January 1989, pp.6–7
The Times, 23 June 1990
First Premium
Civic Trust Awards 1990

Keith Murray in the 1980s

1976
Visitor Centre for St George's Chapel, Windsor Castle
(unexecuted project)
Windsor, Berkshire
Client: The Dean and Chapter of Windsor

1976–80
Conversion and extensions to two houses to provide sheltered housing
Ennerdale Road, Kew Gardens, Surrey
Client: The Abbeyfield Richmond Society

1977
Reordering of St Winefride's Church (RC)
Leyborne Park, Kew Gardens, Surrey
Client: Parish priest of St Winefride's

1977–8
Squash Courts at Cranleigh School
Cranleigh, Surrey
Client: Woodard Schools Ltd

1977–80
Boarders House at Cranleigh School
Cranleigh, Surrey
Client: Woodard Schools Ltd
Conference, October 1980, pp.17–20

1977–81

Upgrading and extension of eight historic boarders' houses at The King's School

Cathedral Precinct, Canterbury, Kent

Client: The King's School

1977–87

Conversion and extension (two phases) of a Victorian school to form Keston College

Keston, Bromley, London

Client: Keston College

1978

Restoration of St Peter's Church, Brockley

Wickham Road, Brockley, London

Client: The Vicar and Parochial Church Council of St Peter's

1978–80

Reordering of St Mary's Church, Mortlake, and upgrading of the Vestry House

Mortlake, London

Client: The Rector and Parochial Church Council of St Mary's

1978–83

Crown Reach apartments, houses and light industry

Grosvenor Road, Westminster, London

(single project partnership with Nicholas Lacey, following adjustments to his winning competition design)

Client: Crown Commissioners and Wates Developments Ltd

1978–83

Boarders' house, day pupils' house, physics laboratory and dining hall extension at The King's School

Cathedral Precinct, Canterbury, Kent

Client: The King's School

Financial Times, 2 June 1980

Architectural Review, September 1983, pp.23–5 and 52–8

Baumeister, Munich, December 1986, pp.48–53

1979–82

Three staff houses for Chelmsford Cathedral

Chelmsford, Essex

Client: The Dean and Chapter of Chelmsford

1979–95

Upgrading and extensions (four phases) at South Weston Cottage

South Weston, Oxfordshire

Client: Alison and Robert Maguire

1980–8

Restorations of the fabric at Lincoln Cathedral

Client: The Dean and Chapter of Lincoln

1981–7

Children's Day Centre in Berlin

(Joachim Schmidt, executive architect)

Paul-Lincke-Ufer, Kreuzberg, Berlin

Client: Internationale Bauausstellung, Berlin

Bauwelt, 1981, IBA-Gruppe Stadterneuerung, Berlin, p.18

Architects' Journal, 15 July 1981, p.99 and 28 October 1981, pp.867–870

Architects' Journal, 12 August 1987, pp.30–41

IBA Projektübersicht, Berlin 1987, pp.344–5

First premium

1981–8

Pedestrianisation and landscaping of three Berlin streets

(in collaboration with Joachim Schmidt)

Paul-Lincke-Ufer, Kreuzberg, Berlin

Client: Internationale Bauausstellung, Berlin

Kita, lettering by Ralph Beyer

1982

Competition entry for seed bank storage and exhibition building at Kew Gardens
(unexecuted project)
Kew, Surrey
Client: Property Services Agency
Architects' Journal, 29 September 1982, pp.42–3

1982–3

Reordering of the east end of All Saints Church, Chevington
Chevington, Suffolk
Client: The Vicar and Parochial Church Council of All Saints
Church Building, Summer 1986, p.36

1982–3

Reordering of St Lawrence's Church, South Weston
South Weston, Oxfordshire
Client: The Vicar and Parochial Church Council of South Weston

1982–6

The Qaboos Pavilion at the Royal Military Academy
Sandhurst, Bracknell, Berkshire
Client: Royal Military Academy

1983–5

Reordering and extension at St Mary's Church, Stow
Stow, Lincolnshire
Client: The Vicar and Parochial Church Council of St Mary's

1983–5

Reordering and extension of the chapel at King's College, Taunton
Taunton, Somerset
Client: Woodard Schools Ltd

1984

St Faith's Junior School
(unexecuted project)
Wandsworth, London
Client: Southwark Diocesan Board of Education

1984–5

Restoration of the Wren Library interior, Lincoln Cathedral
Client: The Dean and Chapter of Lincoln

1984–5

Dance studio for the Laban Centre for Movement and Dance
New Cross, London
Client: University of London, Goldsmith's College

1984–6

Conversion of St Luke's Church, Deptford, to provide a small church and a social centre
Deptford, London
Client: The Vicar and Parochial Church Council of St Nicholas and St Luke

KIng's School, Canterbury, Luxmore House

1984–8

Conversion and extension of existing buildings to provide girls' and staff accommodation, biology and physics laboratories and a day-boys' house at Epsom College

Epsom, Surrey

Client: Epsom College

1985

New kitchen and dining hall at Bedale's School

(unexecuted project)

Steep, Petersfield, Hampshire

Client: Bedales School

1985–6

Barton's Restaurant conversion from coachhouse*

Ealing, London

Client: Standbase Ltd

1985–7

Reordering of St Nicholas' Church, Deptford

Deptford, London

Client: The Vicar and Parochial Church Council of St Nicholas and St Luke

1985–7

Craft, design and technology centre at King's College, Taunton

Taunton, Somerset

Client: Woodard Schools Ltd

1985–7

Reordering of St Paul's Church, Honiton

Honiton, Devon

Client: The Vicar and Parochial Church Council of St Paul's

1985–8

Dennetts Road Estate housing

Peckham, London

Client: Society for Cooperative Dwellings

1985–90

Western extension of St Andrew's Church, North Oxford

Linton Road, Oxford

Client: The Vicar and Parochial Church Council of St Andrew's

Church Building, Summer 1991, pp.24–7

1986–8

All Saints Church, Upper Bucklebury

Upper Bucklebury, Berkshire

Client: The Vicar and Parochial Church Council of St Mary's, Bucklebury

1986–8
Upgrading of student accommodation and staff facilities at Bedales School*
Steep, Petersfield, Hampshire
Client: Bedales School

1986–8
Upgrading and restoration of Ealing Town Hall
Ealing, London
Client: The London Borough of Ealing

1986–9
Chepstow Castle Visitors' Centre
(unexecuted project)
Chepstow, Monmouthshire
Client: CADW
Architects' Journal, 10 September 1986, p.28
Building Design, 12 September 1986
The Architect, December 1986, p.7
First premium
Status: Project abandoned due to government budget cuts after full production information completed

Worcester College, Oxford, Governing Body Room

1986–90
Two quadrangles, student accommodation and conference facilities for Pembroke College, Oxford
Grandpont, Oxford
Client: Pembroke College
Architects' Journal, 11 June 1986, pp.29–49
The Times, 23 June 1990
RIBA Journal, August 1990, pp.6–8

1986–92
First premium

1986–92
Upgrading and extension of Finca Pepe Pedro
Pago de Sarja, Cómpeta, Málaga, Spain
Clients: Alison and Robert Maguire

1987
Student accommodation at Wickham Court
(unexecuted project)
West Wickham, Bromley, London
Client: Schiller International University

1987
Invited competition entry for the British Ambassador's residence in Moscow
(unexecuted project)
Client: HM Government

1987
House extensions
Greenacre, South Weston, Oxfordshire
Client: Mr and Mrs P Lewis

1987–8
Wine and Mousaka restaurant refurbishment
Ealing, London
Client: Katsouris Ltd

Worcester College, Governing Body Room, ceiling

Maguire & Co

1988
Conversion of warehouse to Tea Museum
(unexecuted project)
Bermondsey, London
Client: The Tea Council

1988
Competition entry for a Residential Staff Training Centre for Allied Dunbar
(unexecuted project)
Warnborough, Swindon, Wiltshire
Client: Allied Dunbar Assurance plc
Second premium

1988
Cable-stay footbridge over River Mole
(unexecuted project)
Painshill Park, Cobham, Surrey
Client: Painshill Park Trust

1988
Redesign of Front Quadrangle at Magdalen College, Oxford
(unexecuted project)
Oxford
Client: Magdalen College

1988–90
Governing Body Room, students' accommodation and landscaping at Worcester College, Oxford
Oxford
Client: Worcester College
Building Design, 26 October 1990, p.7, and supplement p.3
Oxcom, Oxford, September/October 1990, p.31
RIBA Journal, March 1991, pp.6–8
First premium

1988–92
Student accommodation for Christ Church and Corpus Christi College, Oxford
Iffley Road, Oxford
Clients: Christ Church and Corpus Christi College
Building Design, 2 June 1989
First premium

1988–93
Reordering of St Mary's Church, Thame
Thame, Oxfordshire
Client: The Vicar and Parochial Church Council of St Mary's
Architects' Journal, 12 December 1996, p.44

1989–91
Reordering of St Mary's Church, Bloxham
Bloxham, Oxfordshire
Client: The Vicar and Parochial Church Council of St Mary's

1989–92
Extensions to Stonesfield County Junior School
Stonesfield, Oxfordshire
Client: Oxfordshire County Council

1989–93
Laboratories, classrooms, CDT centre, staff facilities at The Royal Grammar School
Guildford, Surrey
Client: The Royal Grammar School

1989–93
House for Dr Ahmed Al Malik
(modification of first design by Kenzo Tange)
Riyadh, Saudi Arabia
Client: Dr Ahmed Al Malik

1989–95
University offices, library, central catering, two colleges, conference centre and sports complex for the King Saud University
Al Kassim Campus, Buraydah, Saudi Arabia
Client: King Saud University

1990
House for Dr Osama Al Malik
(unexecuted project)
Riyadh, Saudi Arabia
Client: Dr Ahmed Al Malik
Status: project abandoned during First Gulf War

1990
House for Mr Fahed Al Malik
(unexecuted project)
Riyadh, Saudi Arabia
Client: Mr Fahed Al Malik
Status: project abandoned during First Gulf War

1990
House for Mr Abdulaziz Modiamigh
(unexecuted project)
Riyadh, Saudi Arabia
Client: Mr Abdulaziz Modiamigh
Status: project abandoned during First Gulf War

1990–1
Upgrading of two 17th-century houses to provide student accommodation
Pembroke Street, Oxford
Client: Pembroke College

1990–2
Conversion of the Old Convocation House to a coffee-house
Crypt chamber of St Mary the Virgin Church, Oxford
Client: a trust on behalf of the University of Oxford

1990–2
Conversion of gymnasium to library, and landscaping of main quadrangle at Epsom College
Epsom, Surrey
Client: Epsom College

1991
Competition entry for extensions to the New Court building by Sir Denys Lasdun at Christ's College, Cambridge
(invited: unexecuted project)
King Street, Cambridge
Second premium

1991
The Museum of Scotland, Edinburgh
(competition: unexecuted project)
Chambers Street, Edinburgh
Client: National Museums of Scotland

1991
Competition entry for student accommodation at the University of Leeds
(invited: unexecuted project)
University campus, Leeds
Client: University of Leeds
Second premium

1991

Competition entry for extensions at St John's College, Oxford

(invited: unexecuted project)

Oxford

Client: St John's College

1992

Competition entry for Visitors' Centre at Stonehenge (with Colvin and Moggridge, landscape architects)

(invited: unexecuted project)

Client: English Heritage

Visions for Stonehenge, English Heritage, January 1993

English Heritage commendation

1993

Competition entry for the master plan for the new campus of the University of Cyprus

with Photios Photiou, architect; collaborators Dominic Michaelis (energy) and Hal Moggridge (landscape)

(unexecuted project)

Client: University of Cyprus

Second stage finalist (nine finalists, 156 international entries)

International design ideas for the new campus, University of Cyprus, January 1997, pp.38–9

Status: drawings retained for study by university staff architect, and never returned

1993

Master plan for the Abha Campus of the King Saud University

(unexecuted project)

Abha, Saudi Arabia

Client: King Saud University

Status: plan accepted but new site donated, and client obliged to re-tender appointment internationally

1994

Conference and reception facilities at the British Consulate, Jeddah

(unexecuted project)

Jeddah, Saudi Arabia

Client: HM Government

1994–5

Swimming pool, community facilities and extension of hall at the British Embassy, Saudi Arabia

Riyadh, Saudi Arabia

Client: HM Government

1994–5

Restoration of Radley Hall (1725) at Radley College

(in collaboration with Alison Maguire, architectural historian)

Abingdon, Oxfordshire

Client: Radley College

1994–6

Reordering of the chapel of Burnham Abbey

Taplow, Buckinghamshire

Client: The Society of the Precious Blood (C of E)

Architects' Journal, 12 December 1996, p.45

1994–7

Thirteen university buildings for the Abha Campus of King Saud University, including administration, libraries, catering, three colleges, women students' accommodation, mosque and lecture theatres

(unexecuted project)

Abha, Saudi Arabia

Client: King Saud University

Status: all projects approved, but new university site donated, obliging client to re-tender appointment internationally

1995–6

Conversion of barn and classrooms to library at Radley College

Abingdon, Oxfordshire

Client: Radley College

1995–7

Queen's Court laboratories and classrooms at Radley College

Abingdon, Oxfordshire

Client: Radley College

RIBA Journal, September 1995, pp.26–7

RIBA Journal, December 1997, pp.44–9

First premium

1996

Competition entry for the Visitor Facilities at Norwich Cathedral

(invited: unexecuted project)

Client: The Dean and Chapter of Norwich

Status: competition results not announced; no publication allowed; drawings not returned

1996–8

Private housing estate at Muir of Ord

Beulah, Muir of Ord, Inverness

Client: Cornerstone Limited

Status: five houses built, but land then sold on

1996–2000

Reordering of Greyfriars Church, Reading

Reading, Berkshire

Client: The Vicar and Parochial Church Council of Greyfriars

Church Building, issue 70 2001, pp.45–8

1997

Further reordering (see 1962) of St Thomas's Church, Heptonstall to provide facilities to Pennine Way walkers

(unexecuted project)

Heptonstall, Hebden Bridge, West Yorkshire

Client: The Vicar and Parochial Church Council of St Thomas's

1997–8

Upgrading and extension of classrooms, and new studio theatre, at Radley College

Abingdon, Oxfordshire

Client: Radley College

1997–9

Reordering of the chapel of St Pega's Hermitage, and upgrading of the retreat house*

Peakirk, Peterborough

Client: The Society of the Precious Blood (C of E)

Status: the Hermitage is now a private residence

Church Building, March/April 1999, pp.45–6

1997–2000

Theatre, art gallery and sports hall at Dormston Comprehensive School

Sedgley, West Midlands

Client: Dudley Borough Council and Dormston School, in association with the National Lottery Arts and Sports Funds

RIBA Journal, May 2001, pp.39–44

1998

Competition entry for the Cyprus Law Courts

(unexecuted project)

(jointly with Photios Photiou, architect)

Client: Cyprus government

1998–9

House extension and upgrading

Kingston Blount, Oxfordshire

Client: Mr and Mrs J Donaldson

1998–2000

Restoration and conversion to a house of Monks Barn

North Hinksey, Oxfordshire
Client: The Rev & Mrs D McNeile

1998–2001
Students' houses for Jesus College, Oxford
Jesus College sports field, Herbert Close, East
Oxford
Client: Jesus College
RIBA Journal, February 2002, pp.34–40

1998–2001
**Reordering of St Michael and All Angels
Church, Eastbourne***
Willingdon, Eastbourne, East Sussex
Client: The Vicar and Parochial Church Council
of St Michael and All Angels
Status: further key furnishings have since been
carried out by others

1998–2002
Reordering of St Helen's Church, Abingdon
Abingdon, Oxfordshire
Client: The Vicar and Parochial Church Council
of St Helen's
Robert Maguire, 'Seats in church', Trevor Cooper
and Sarah Brown (eds), *Pews, benches and chairs:
church seating in English parish churches from
the fourteenth century to the present*, London, the
Ecclesiological Society 2011, pp.335–50

1999–2001
**Extension and upgrading of the Old Rectory
at Wotton Underwood**
Wotton Underwood, Buckinghamshire
Client: Mr and Mrs S Laidlaw

1999–2001
**Reordering of the private chapel in the
Bishop's Palace**
Peterborough
Client: The Bishop of Peterborough with the
Church Commissioners

1999–2001
Ecumenical church and community centre
Fairford Leys, Aylesbury, Buckinghamshire
Client: local churches: URC, C of E, and RC

1999–2003
**Upgrading, conversion and extensions at
Jesus College, Oxford to provide student
accommodation and Junior Common Room**
Oxford
Client: Jesus College, Oxford

2000–4
Oxford University Club
Mansfield Road, Oxford
Client: University of Oxford
(scheme carried through by Maguire & Co after
Robert Maguire's retirement)

2000–6
Reordering of St Mary's Church, Hitcham
Hitcham, Burnham, Buckinghamshire
Client: The Vicar and Parochial Church Council
of St Mary's
(scheme carried through by JBKS Architects after
Robert Maguire's retirement)

2001
Reordering of All Saints Church, Marlow
(unexecuted project)
Marlow, Buckinghamshire
Client: The Vicar and Parochial Church Council
of All Saints

2001
**Reordering and extension of Holy Trinity
Church and Henry Martin Memorial Hall,
Cambridge**
(unexecuted project)
Market Street, Cambridge
Client: The Vicar and Parochial Church Council
of Holy Trinity

2001–3
Reordering of St Peter's & St Paul's Church, Buckingham
Castle Hill, Buckingham, Buckinghamshire
Client: The Vicar and Parochial Church Council
of St Peter and St Paul

2001–4
Sports Pavilion at Radley College
Radley, Abingdon, Oxfordshire
Client: Radley College
(scheme carried through by Maguire & Co after
Robert Maguire's retirement)

2001–4
St Boniface's Church, Plymouth
Percy Street, St Budeaux, Plymouth, Devon
Client: The Vicar and Parochial Church Council
of St Boniface's
(scheme carried through by Maguire & Co after
Robert Maguire's retirement)
Church Building, November/December 2004,
pp.18–21

2001–4
St Thomas the Apostle Church, Plymouth, and conversion of house to parish rooms and offices
Royal Navy Avenue, Keyham, Plymouth
Client: The Vicar and Parochial Church Council
of St Thomas's
(scheme carried through by Maguire & Co after
Robert Maguire's retirement)

2002
Reordering of St Peter's Church, Burnham
(unexecuted project)
Burnham, Buckinghamshire
Client: The Vicar and Parochial Church Council
of St Peter's

2002–7
St Bede's Church, Basingstoke (RC)
Popley, Basingstoke, Hampshire
(church and atrium by Robert Maguire; house
and parish rooms by JBKS Architects)
Client: The Roman Catholic Diocese of
Portsmouth
(scheme carried through by JBKS Architects after
Robert Maguire's retirement)
Church Times, 17 August 2007

2003–8
Reordering of St Mary's Church, Thatcham
Thatcham, Berkshire
Client: The Vicar and Parochial Church Council
of St Mary's

2003
Hard and soft landscaping of the Courts at Sherborne School
Sherborne, Dorset
(unexecuted project)
Client: Sherborne School

2003–5
Upgrading of Victorian school hall at Sherborne School to auditorium status
Sherborne, Dorset
Client: Sherborne School
(scheme carried through by JBKS Architects after
Robert Maguire's retirement)

2003–6
Restoration of 17th-century hall at Sherborne School
Sherborne, Dorset
Client: Sherborne School
(scheme carried through by JBKS Architects after
Robert Maguire's retirement)

Keith Murray and Joachim Schmidt Architekten Berlin

1984–7
Refurbishment and extensions to Adolf-Damaschke-Schule
Skalitzer Strasse, Kreuzberg, Berlin
Client: Internationale Bauausstellung, Berlin
Building Design, 27 July 1984, p.1
IBA Stadterneuerung: Berichte zur Stadterneuerung in Kreuzberg: Schulprojekt SO36 "Kiezschule", IBA and STERN: Berlin, December 1991

Conversion of electricity substation into an Arts and Social Centre
(unexecuted project)
Paul-Lincke-Ufer, Kreuzberg, Berlin
Client: STERN
Status: project aborted after German reunification

Refurbishment and restructuring of Gustav Stresemann Grundschule
Tempelhofer Ufer, Kreuzberg, Berlin
(unexecuted project)
Kreuzberg, West Berlin
Client: STERN
Status: project aborted after German reunification

Replanning and extension of Adolf Glasbrenner Grundschule
(unexecuted project)
Hagelberger Strasse, Kreuzberg, West Berlin
Client: STERN
Status: project aborted after German reunification

Keith Murray

1999–2000
Redesign and extension of 'Olivers' wholefood shop
(with Brian Hendry Architect)
Station Approach, Kew Gardens, Surrey
Client: Sara Novakovic

1995–2000
Reordering of St Mary the Virgin Church
Lewisham High Street, Lewisham, London
Client: The Vicar and Parochial Church Council of St Mary's
(includes the commission of a carved Madonna and Child)

1998–2001
Reordering of the Barn Church (St Philip and All Saints)
(with Brian Hendry Architect)
Atwood Avenue, Kew, Surrey
Client: The Vicar and Parochial Church Council of St Philip and All Saints

1997–2000
Improvements to Old Priory Buildings, Monmouth
(with Batterham Matthews Design, Architects and Surveyors)
Monk Street, Monmouth
Client: The Vicar and Parochial Church Council of St Mary's, Monmouth
Church Building, March/April 2006, Issue 98, pp.36–9

Robert Maguire

2004–6
Three-generation house
Hopewater House, Ettrickbridge, Selkirk, Scottish Borders
Client: Robert and Alison Maguire, Mathew and Lucy Williams

2005
Redesign of the setting of the 1510 Amsterdam retable in the chapel of Radley College
(architect/architectural historian collaboration by Robert and Alison Maguire)
Abingdon, Oxfordshire
Client: Radley College

Appendix: '5 Lessons' from the Humanes Bauen exhibition catalogue

Notes

I. We are interested in building for people, not in producing "Architecture" primarily. If you serve people well, the reflection of life which results tends to produce architectural character. It is that way round.

2. We are interested in places as well as people. The place we build in has an influence on the kind of building we design. We see this also as a kind of respect for people. Because the place is also a reflection of the lives of people living in it – even when it is ugly, it means something to them.

3. We are interested in scale; few modern buildings are "in scale" with people. This is not merely a matter of size; a single-storey building can be "out of scale"; and a ten-storey building "in scale".

4. We have usually worked on very low budgets. We think you can build "for people" with very little money. It is a matter of getting the values right. A lot therefore depends on the people we are building for.

5. *Traditional architecture*: We are much influenced by this ("country" or "vernacular" building, rather than stylistic traditional architecture) but it is, we feel, important to say *in what way*. It is *not* a style, or a series of forms, to be copied. We use similar forms, when they are *appropriate* to a situation; the similarities are frequent because vernacular building has evolved around the idea of appropriateness.

Lesson 1: it shows a great straightforwardness in solving problems. Or an "economy", in more than money-terms.

Lesson 2: it shows how simplicity can build up into apparent complexity, by being consistently applied. The lesson is, that character emerges, and is not *imposed*.

Lesson 3: it shows a human scale.

Lesson 4: it shows how buildings can be images of human life, by serving life well. The buildings are then, in some way, lovable.

Lesson 5: it shows how to use materials – any materials. Therefore you can learn how to use a new material, by being "direct" in the same way. We do not often use obviously "traditional" materials, but we are aware that our buildings often have a feeling of some tradition behind them (even if made of concrete blocks and asbestos slates).

Robert Maguire & Keith Murray, 1975

"We have an ordinary conviction that architecture is about people ... not merely that its purpose is to serve people at a high level of usefulness and comfort, plus some extra ingredient which makes it look nice. Architecture is concerned with human need ..."

"This then is what we have clarified as our basic conviction: that the primary object of the creative architectural process is to achieve–, to use Lethaby's phrase – "nearness to need". We have established this as a kind of lifeline, by which we have found we can return to a point of reference and take our bearings again amid the confusion and complexity of the architectural currents in which we have to work."

"It is essential to recognise and accept one's feelings or intuitions as positive, otherwise the architect is denying himself the very thing which most distinguishes his activity from that of others concerned in the building process: *he is the one who can articulate built farm so that it bears the imprint of human life and human feeling.* It may be mainly these unformulated areas of his understanding which will relate the building, as a symbol of feeling, to the life it serves."

"We have evolved a body of ideas about spaces and materials and structure and the way they work in and through a building or an environment to affect people's lives. This has been derived mostly from observation of what these things do, negatively and positively, in the scene around us."

"Modern architects look at vernacular buildings and admire them, but put them into a bracket which has no relevance, because it does not conform to their image of what modern architecture 'ought' to be like. This kind of inhibition, which causes possibilities to be rejected before they are even considered, puts an appalling restriction on our inventive powers. It also limits our openness to what we observe."

"On the low budgets to which we usually have to work, we aim for a high standard of ordinariness, using cheap materials carefully detailed so that the built form is convincing as something built as well as a form, which we find gives cheap materials a heightened value."

"We feel that if you concern yourself to design an environment which shows respect for people, which allows them to live, they will in turn respect the environment."

Extract from Robert Maguire, 'Nearness to Need',
RIBAJ, April 1971, pp. 140–148.

Architectural staff list

After the first three years, the size of the practice varied from 5 to 12 architectural staff.
Staff turnover was low, over the entire 46 years' total of the two firms.
Those who became Associates are marked †
Directors (not all contemporaneous) of Maguire & Co are marked *

Robert Maguire & Keith Murray

Martin Andrews
Jeremy Bell
Chris Bennett
Alan Berman
Robin Bishop
Charles Brackenbury
Steve Bradshaw
Jennifer Evans
Michael Evans
Martin Eyre
Frederico Fernandez
Nicola Foot
Brian Hendry
Theo Hopkins
Paul Hyett
Arno Jobst †
Warren Kelly
Martha Maguire
Jill Manson †
John Martin
Peter Martin
Charlie McCallum
Paul Middleton
Nicholas Midgley
Andrew Parfitt
Ross Porter †
Liz Pride
Gordon Russell
Ian Salisbury
Rajindar Singh †
Simon Smith
Andrew Thorneywork
Kai Tse
Oliver Tyler
Ekkehard Weisner
Adam Whiteley

Maguire & Co

Jeremy Bell *
Steve Bradshaw
Mike Cleary
Jill Ewbank
Nicola Foot
Nicola Macdonald
Jill Manson *
Nicholas Midgley
Huw Owen
Christopher Platt
Connie Platt
John Radice
Ifor Rhys
Cliff Robinson
Adrian Rouse
Ian Salisbury *
Kelvin Sampson *
Rajindar Singh *
Charles Taylor
Andrew Thorneywork *
Eduardo Ralita Uriate
David Welbourne *
Edward Williams
Luke Williamson
Yolande Wyer

Bibliography

Books, journals and articles consulted

Gerald Adler, 'Little Boxes', in *Scale: imagination, perception and practice in architecture*, Gerald Adler, Timothy Brittain-Catlin and Gordana Fontana-Giusti, (eds), (Abingdon: Routledge, 2012).

Gerald Adler, 'Something out of the "Ordinary"', in *The Cultural Role of Architecture*, Paul Emmons, John Hendrix, Jane Lomholt, (eds), (Abingdon: Routledge, 2012).

Theodor Adorno and Max Horkheimer, *Dialectic of Enlightenment: philosophical fragments* (Stanford, CA: Stanford University Press, 2002), Gunzelin Schmid Noerr, (eds); trans. Edmund Jephcott.

Christopher Alexander, *Notes on the Synthesis of Form*, (Cambridge, MA: Harvard University Press, 1964).

Christopher Alexander, *The Timeless Way of Building*, (New York: Oxford University Press, 1979).

Christopher Alexander, Sara Ishikawa, Murray Silverstein with others, *A Pattern Language: towns, buildings, construction*, (New York: Oxford University Press, 1977).

Bryan Appleyard, *The Pleasures of Peace: art and imagination in post-war Britain*, (London: Faber and Faber, 1989).

George Baird, '"Criticality" and its Discontents, in *The new Architectural Pragmatism: Harvard Design Magazine Reader 5*, William S. Saunder, (ed.), (Minneapolis, MN: University of Minnesota Press, 2007).

Reyner Banham, *Guide to Modern Architecture*, (London: Architectural Press, 1962).

Reyner Banham, *The New Brutalism: ethic or aesthetic?*, (London: The Architectural Press, 1966).

Reyner Banham, 'A modern church on liturgical principles', *Architectural Review*, December 1960, p.400.

Michael Benedikt, *For an Architecture of Reality*, (New York: Lumen, 1987).

John Berger, *Ways of Seeing*, (London: BBC and Harmondsworth: Penguin, 1972).

Alan Berman (ed.), *Jim Stirling and the Red Trilogy: three radical buildings*, (London: Frances Lincoln, 2010).

Peter Blundell Jones, '1: In search of authenticity', *Architects' Journal*, 30 October 1991, pp.25–30; '2:'Tectonic authenticity', *Architects' Journal*, 6 November 1991, pp.32–6; '3: Social authenticity', *Architects' Journal*, 4 December 1991, pp.22–5; '4: Politics of Post-Modern despair', *Architects' Journal*, 8 and 15, January 1992, pp.29–32.

Louis Bouyer, *Life and Liturgy*, (London: Sheed and Ward, 1956).

Louis Bouyer, *Liturgy and Architecture*, (Notre Dame, IN: University of Notre Dame Press, 1967).

Ronald William Brunskill, *Illustrated handbook of vernacular architecture*, (London: Faber, 1970).

Nicholas Bullock, *Building the Post-war World: modern architecture and reconstruction in Britain*, (London and New York: Routledge, 2002).

John Carter, 'To endless years the same?', *Architects' Journal*, 6 October 1976, pp.630–661.

Ernst Cassirer, *The Philosophy of Symbolic Forms. Volume 4, The Metaphysics of Symbolic Forms*, (New Haven and London: Yale University Press, 1996), John Michael Krois and Donald Philip Verene, (eds); trans. John Michael Kroi).

Serge Chermayeff and Christopher Alexander, *Community and Privacy: toward a new architecture of humanism*, (Harmondsworth: Penguin, 1966).

Alec Clifton-Taylor, *The Pattern of English Building*, (London: Faber, 1972).

Gilbert Cope (ed.), *Making the Building serve the Liturgy: studies in the re-ordering of churches*, (London: Mowbray, 1962).

Gordon Cullen, *Townscape*, (London: Architectural Press, 1961).

Colin Cunningham, *Stones of Witness: church architecture and function*, (Stroud: Sutton, 1999).

Justus Dahinden, *New Trends in Church Architecture*, (London: Studio, 1967).

John Gordon Davies, *The Secular Use of Church Buildings*, (London: SCM Press, 1968).

Gregory Dix, *The Shape of the Liturgy*, (London: Dacre, 1943).

John Eastwick-Field and John Stillman, *The Design and Practice of Joinery*, (London: Architectural Press and TRADA, 1958, drawings by Robert Maguire).

Lionel Esher, *A Broken Wave: The Rebuilding of England 1940–1980*, (London: Allen Lane, 1981).

Design Guide for Residential Areas, Essex County Council, 1973.

Richard Foster, *Discovering English Churches*, (London: BBC, 1981).

Kenneth Frampton, 'Towards a Critical Regionalism: Six points for an architecture of resistance', in *Anti-Aesthetic: essays on postmodern culture*, Hal Foster, (ed.), (Seattle: Bay Press, 1983).

Maxwell Fry, *Horizon*, May 1946.

Robert Philip Gibbons, 'St Paul's, Bow Common: a voice in the wilderness', *Church Building*, Winter 1989/90, pp.14–15.

Richard Giles, *Repitching the Tent: re-ordering the church building for worship and mission in the new millennium*, (Norwich: Canterbury Press, 1996).

Natalia Ginzburg, *The Little Virtues*, (Manchester: Carcanet, 1985, trans. Dick Davis).

Andor Gomme and Alison Maguire, *Design and Planning the Country House: from castle donjons to Palladian boxes*, (London and New Haven: Yale University Press, 2008).

Peter Hammond, 'A Liturgical Brief', *Architectural Review*, April 1958.

Peter Hammond, *Liturgy and Architecture*, (London: Barry and Rockliff, 1960).

Peter Hammond (ed.), *Towards a Church Architecture*, (London: Architectural Press, 1962).

Alexandra Harris, *Romantic Moderns*, (London: Thames & Hudson, 2010).

Tanya Harrod, *The Crafts in Britain in the 20th Century*, (New Haven, CT and London: Published for The Bard Graduate Center for Studies in the Decorative Arts by Yale University Press, 1999).

Elain Harwood, 'Liturgy and Architecture: The Development of the Centralised Eucharistic Space', *The Twentieth Century Church, Twentieth Century Architecture 3, The Journal of the Twentieth Century Society* (1998), pp.49–74.

Edwin Heathcote and Laura Moffat, *Contemporary Church Architecture*, (Chichester: Wiley, 2007).

Arthur Gabriel Hebert, *Liturgy and Society: the function of the church in the modern world*, (London: Faber and Faber, 1935).

Dave Hickey, 'Dialectical Utopias', *Harvard Design Magazine 4*, Winter/ Spring 1998, pp.8–13.

Andrew Higgott, *Mediating Modernism: architectural cultures in Britain*, (Abingdon: Routledge, 2007).

Ivan Illich, *Deschooling Society*, (London: Calder and Boyars, 1971).

Lesley Jackson, *'Contemporary': architecture and interiors of the 1950s*, (London: Phaidon, 1994).

Tom Jarman, *Retrospective: Maguire & Murray*, (University of Bath, Department of Architecture and Civil Engineering, 2006), (unpublished dissertation, Master of Architecture).

George Everard Kidder Smith, *The New Churches of Europe*, (London: The Architectural Press, 1964).

Richard Kieckhefer, *Theology in Stone: church architecture from Byzantium to Berkeley*, (New York, NY: Oxford University Press, 2004).

Osbert Lancaster, *Pillar to Post: English architecture without tears*, (London: John Murray, 1938).

Royston Landau, *New Directions in British Architecture*, (London: Studio Vista, 1968).

Suzanne Langer, *Philosophy in a New Key*, (Cambridge, MA: Harvard University Press, 1942).

Suzanne Langer, *Feeling and Form*, (New York: Scribner's, 1953).

Philip Larkin, *The Less Deceived*, (London: Faber & Faber, 1955).

Le Corbusier, *Towards a New Architecture*, (London: Architectural Press; 1927), trans. Frederick Etchells. Originally published in French as Le Corbusier (Charles Edouard Jeanneret), *Vers une Architecture*, (Paris: Georges Crès, 1923).

Geradus van der Leeuw, *Sacred and Profane Beauty: the holy in art*, (Oxford: Oxford University Press, 1963), trans. David E. Green, first published in Dutch in 1932.

Claude Lichtenstein and Thomas Schregenberger (eds), *As Found: the discovery of the ordinary*, (Baden, Switzerland: Lars Müller, 2001).

Vladimir Lossky, *Essai sur la Théologie Mystique de l'Eglise d'Orient*, (Paris: Aubier, 1944).

Charles Lutyens, 'Wrestling with Angels: a reflection by Charles Lutyens', *Church Building* Spring 1990, pp.18–21 (with an introduction by Keith Murray).

Donlyn Lyndon, Charles W. Moore, Patrick J. Quinn and Sim van Der Ryn, 'Toward Making Places', *Landscape 12*, No. 1 (Autumn 1962).

Leslie Martin, Ben Nicholson and Naum
Gabo (eds), *Circle: international survey
of constructivist art*, (London: Faber &
Faber, 1937).

Raymond McGrath, *Glass in Architecture
and Decoration*, (London:
Architectural Press, 1937).

Nigel Melhuish, 'Church building in the
'sixties', *The Architects' Journal*, 8 July
1970, pp.70–71.

Jeremy Melvin, 'Heart of class', *RIBA
Journal*, May 2001, pp.38–44.

Edward Mills, *The Modern Church*,
(London: Architectural Press, 1956).

Iris Murdoch, *Under the Net*, (London:
Chatto & Windus, 1954).

Osbert Lancaster, *Homes Sweet Homes*,
(London: John Murray, 1939).

Ian Nairn, *Nairn's London*,
(Harmondsworth: Penguin, 1966).

Paul Oliver, *Dwellings: the house across the
world*, (Oxford: Phaidon, 1987).

Paul Oliver (ed.), *Encyclopedia of
Vernacular Architecture of the World*,
(Cambridge: Cambridge University
Press, 1997).

Wolfgang Pehnt, *Rudolf Schwarz
(1897–1961): Architekt einer anderen
Moderne*, (Stuttgart: Hatje, 1997).

John and Jane Penoyre, *Houses in the
Landscape: a regional study of
vernacular building styles in England
and Wales*, (London: Faber, 1978).

*(Plowden Report: 1967) Children and
their Primary Schools. A Report of
the Central Advisory Council for
Education (England)*, (London: Her
Majesty's Stationery Office, 1967).

Kenneth Powell, *Powell & Moya: twentieth
century architects*, (London: RIBA
Publishing, 2009).

Alan Powers, *Britain: modern architec-
tures in history*, (London: Reaktion,
2009).

Alan Powers, *Aldington, Craig and
Collinge: twentieth century architects*,
(London: RIBA Publishing, 2009).

Marcel Proust, *A Remembrance of Things
Past: Swann's Way*, (London: Chatto &
Windus, 1957).

James Maude Richards, *The Functional
Tradition in Early Industrial Buildings*,
(London: Architectural Press, 1958,
with photographs by Eric de Maré).

Johnny Rodger, *Gillespie, Kidd & Coia:
architecture 1956–1987*, (Glasgow:
RIAS and The Lighthouse, 2007).

Andrew Saint, *Towards a Social
Architecture: the role of school-building
on post-war England*, (New Haven and
London: Yale University Press, 1987).

Dominic Sandbrook, *Never Had It So
Good: a history of Britain from Suez
to the Beatles*, (London: Little, Brown,
2005).

Dominic Sandbrook, *White Heat: a
history of Britain in the Swinging
Sixties* (London: Little, Brown, 2006).

Rudolf Schwarz, *The Church Incarnate:
the sacred function of Christian
architecture*, (Chicago: Henry
Regnery, 1958), trans. Cynthia Harris.
Originally published as *Vom Bau
der Kirche*, (Heidelberg: Lambert
Schneider, 1938).

Rudolf Schwarz, *Kirchenbau: Welt vor der
Schwelle*, (Heidelberg: Kerle, 1960).

Frederic J. Schwartz, *Blind Spots: critical
theory and the history of art in
twentieth-century Germany*, (New
Haven and London: Yale University
Press, 2005).

Rainer Senn, 'Il a planté sa tente parmi nous: le problème des églises économiques', *L'Art Sacré*, No. 11-12, July/August 1958.

Rainer Senn, 'The Spirit of Poverty', *Churchbuilding 9*, (196), p.63, trans. Keith Harrison. Originally published as Rainer Senn, 'La Transparence de la Pauvreté', *L'Art Sacré*, No. 5-6, January/February 1958.

Peter Frederick Smith, *Third Millennium Churches*, (London: Galliard, 1972).

Alison and Peter Smithson, 'The New Brutalism', *Architectural Design*, January 1955.

Alison Smithson (ed.), *Team 10 Primer: with additional reprints from various issues of Architectural Design*, (London: Studio Vista, 1968).

Martin Steinmann, *Forme forte: Ecrits/Schriften 1972–2002*, (Basel, Boston and Berlin: Birkhäuser, 2003).

Wolfgang Jean Stock, *Christliche Sakralbauten in Europa seit 1950/Christian Sacred Buildings in Europe since 1950*, (Munich/Berlin/London/New York: Prestel, 2004).

John Summerson, *Georgian London*, (London: Pleiades, 1945).

John Thomas, 'An Architect and his Churches', *Church Building*, March/April 1996, pp.6–7.

Colin Ward, 'Accidental heroes', *New Society*, 8 May 1978, p.374.

Michael Webb, *Architecture in Britain Today*, (Feltham: Hamlyn/Country Life, 1969).

Ulrich Weisner, (ed.), *Humanes Bauen*, exhib. cat., Kunsthalle Bielefeld, 15 June–3 August 1975.

Rudolf Wittkower, *Architectural Principles in the Age of Humanism*, (London: Warburg Institute, 1949).

Frank Lloyd Wright, *An Autobiography*, (New York: Duell, Sloan and Pearce, 1943).

Francis Reginald Stevens Yorke, *The Modern House in England*, (London: Architectural Press, 1937).

Interviews

Robert Maguire interviewed by Linda Sandino, 2004, 'Architects' Lives', 'National Life Stories Collection', British Library Sound Archive, reference F14761/4, F14905/7, F14957/9 (recorded February–April 2004).

Published texts by Robert Maguire, Keith Murray and jointly

Robert Maguire and Peter Matthews, 'The Ironbridge at Coalbrookdale: a reassessment', *Architectural Association Journal (AAJ)*, July–August 1958, pp.30–45.

Robert Maguire and Keith Murray, 'The architect must ask questions', *Church Buildings Today* No. 1, October 1960, pp.3–4.

Robert Maguire and Keith Murray, 'Architecture and Christian Meanings', *Studia Liturgica*, June 1962.

Robert Maguire and Keith Murray, 'Anglican Church in Stepney', *Churchbuilding*, No. 7, October 1962, p.18.

Robert Maguire (under the pseudonym Alfred Roberts), Open letter to the church furnishers, *Churchbuilding*, No. 7, October 1962, pp.24–5.

Robert Maguire, 'Meaning and Understanding', in *Towards a Church Architecture*, Peter Hammond, (ed.), (London: Architectural Press, 1962), pp.69–77.

Keith Murray, 'Material Fabric and Symbolic Pattern', in *Towards a Church Architecture*, Peter Hammond, (ed.), (London: Architectural Press, 1962), pp.78–90.

Robert Maguire, 'Seats in church', *Churchbuilding*, No. 12, April 1964, pp.18–22.

Robert Maguire and Keith Murray, *Modern Churches of the World*, (London: Dutton Vista, 1965).

Robert Maguire and Keith Murray, 'Expandable Churches: a project', *Churchbuilding*, No. 17, January 1966, p.5.

Robert Maguire and Keith Murray, 'Specification in practice: concrete blocks', *RIBA Journal*, March 1970, pp.117–21.

Robert Maguire and Keith Murray, 'Setting up in practice', *Architects' Journal*, 20 January 1971, pp.143–6.

Robert Maguire, 'Nearness to need', *RIBA Journal*, April 1971, pp.140–8.

Robert Maguire, 'Architecture with a small a', *AC Review*, Zurich, April 1976.

Robert Maguire, 'Designing 'place'', *RIBA Journal*, July 1976, p.275.

Robert Maguire, 'The Value of Tradition', *Architects' Journal*, 18 August 1976, pp.292–5 (edited text of 'Something out of the Ordinary?', London, RIBA Publications, 1977).

Keith Murray, 'Concern for the craft', *Architectural Review*, October 1976, p.205.

Robert Maguire, 'Something out of the ordinary?' in *Architecture: Opportunities, Achievements. A report of the annual conference of the Royal Institute of British Architects held at the University of Hull, 14–17 July 1976*, Barbara Goldstein, (ed.), (London: RIBA Publications, 1977).

Keith Murray, 'People and places: St Augustine's, Tunbridge Wells', *The Clergy Review*, January 1978.

Robert Maguire, 'The Art of Architecture', 'Stimulus Papers: "The making of an architect" conference', University of York, 21–22 March 1978.

Robert Maguire, 'Vom Wert der Tradition', *Baumeister*, Munich, February 1980, pp.133–6.

Robert Maguire, 'A conflict between art and life?' in *Architecture for People*, Byron Mikellides, (ed.), (London: Studio Vista, 1980).

Robert Maguire, 'A service to the profession?', *Architects' Journal*, 29 September 1982, p.43.

Robert Maguire, 'The quality of simplicity', *The Fibrecement Review* ac107, April 1983, p.5.

Robert Maguire, 'Vom Wert der Tradition' *Hugo Häring in seiner Zeit – Bauen in unserer Zeit*, Claus-Wilhelm Hoffman, (ed.), Stadt Biberach, Biberach an der Riss, Stuttgart, 1983, pp.141–8 and *Baumeister* Munich February 1980 pp.133–6

Robert Maguire, 'A tribute to the vicar of St Paul's', *Church Building*, Winter 1989/90, p.15.

Keith Murray, 'St Paul's Bow Common (2). The Mosaics: Introduction by Keith Murray', *Church Building*, Spring 1990, p.18.

Robert Maguire, '"Frontis" review of the National Gallery Sainsbury Wing', *RIBA Journal*, September 1991, p.12.

Robert Maguire, '"Frontis" review of Bracken House, London', *RIBA Journal*, July 1992, p.6.

Robert Maguire, 'In defence of modernism', *Association of Christians in Planning & Architecture (ACPA) newsletter*, 1984.

Robert Maguire, 'Conservation in architecture: a failure of understanding', *Church Building*, November/December 1994, pp.31–3.

Robert Maguire, 'Continuity and modernity in the holy place', *Journal of the Society of Architectural Historians*, 1995.

Robert Maguire, 'The Reordering of Churches: what is it to be radical?', (unpublished paper read at the Liturgy North conference organised by the Diocese of Wakefield, May 1996).

Robert Maguire, 'Radical strategic planning for tertiary education', PEB Exchange (OECD), Paris, February 1997.

Robert Maguire, 'Conservation and diverging philosophies', *Journal of Architectural Conservation*, March 1997, pp.7–18.

Keith Murray, 'Painting, Drawing and Teaching' (tribute to Peter Hammond), *Church Building*, May/June 1999, p.10.

Robert Maguire, 'Architectural Theory and the New Churches Research Group' (tribute to Peter Hammond), *Church Building*, May/June 1999, pp.11–12.

Robert Maguire, 'Greyfriars church, Reading', *Church Building*, issue 70, 2001, pp.45–8.

Robert Maguire, 'Church design since 1950', *Ecclesiology Today*, January 2002, pp.2–14.

Robert Maguire, 'Recollections of the early days of the St Paul's project', Kenneth Leech, 'Father Gresham Kirkby: priest of the Kingdom of God', *Anglo-Catholic History Society*, 2009 (Appendix 4).

Robert Maguire, 'Seats in church', *Pews, benches and chairs: church seating in English parish churches from the fourteenth century to the present*, Trevor Cooper and Sarah Brown, (eds), London, the Ecclesiological Society, 2011, pp.335–50.

Index

Page numbers in italics refer to illustrations

Picture Credits

The author and publisher have made every effort to contact copyright holders and will be happy to correct, in subsequent editions, any errors or omissions that are brought to their attention.

James O. Davies, English Heritage:
Front cover, 20, 27, 28, 42 (bottom), 43 (top), 63, 99 (bottom), 102 (top), 103 (both), 136, 144, 174
Martin Charles:
Frontispiece (ii), 6, 102 (bottom), 154 (bottom), 155, 184
Robert Maguire:
vi, 9, 10 (both), 11 (both), 12, 16, 17, 18 (both), 19 (both), 21, 26, 30 (all), 31, 38 (bottom), 41 (all), 46 (both), 47 , 48 (top), 50, 51 (both), 53, 54 (bottom), 55, 56 (all), 58 (both), 59 (both), 62, 64 (bottom), 65 (both), 66, 72, 77, 79 (left), 80 (all), 86, 90, 95, 96, 97, 98, 99 (top), 101, 102 (middle), 104, 110, 111 (bottom), 112, 113, 114 (both), 115, 117 (both), 118 (both), 119, 120 (both), 122, 125, 128, 129 (bottom), 130, 133, 134 (both), 135 (both), 138, 141, 149, 150, 152, 154 (top), 157 (both), 158 (top), 159 (bottom), 160, 165 (both), 169 (top), 174, 175, 185, 186
Watts & Co:
13, 14 (top right)
Gilbert Shevel, Watts & Co:
14 (top left)
Tim Porter:
34
Robert Maguire & Keith Murray:
91
John Whybrow:
43 (bottom right), 68, 73 (top and middle), 88, 89
Keith Murray:
xi, 24 (all), 36, 38 (top), 43 (bottom left), 48 (bottom), 54 (top), 60, 61, 76 (top), 100 (both), 129 (top), 160, 162, 163, 164 (both), 166, 169 (bottom two), 179

Norman Gold:
20, 78, 79 (left), 82, 83 (both)
Rainer Senn:
85 (all)
Sam Lambert:
87, 89
Peter Cook:
123 (both)
Nicholas Meyjes:
127, 131
Architectural Press/ RIBA Library Photographs Collection:
8, back cover
Charlotte Wood:
63, 64 (top), 126, 136, 137, 140 (both), 142, 143, 144, 153, 158 (bottom), 159 (top)
Ralph Beyer:
183
Richard Davies:
106, 111 (top)
Reginald Hugo de Burgh Galway:
73 (bottom)
Bill Toomey/ Architectural Press/ RIBA Library Photographs Collection:
175
Lewis & Randall:
68
Stewart Galloway:
92
Richard Einzig/ Arcaid:
94 (both)
Gerald Adler:
42 (top), 79 (right)
Ian Salisbury:
172
Journal of Ecclesiological Society:
78